SO, YOU WANT TO START YOUR OWN BUSINESS

Everything You Ever Wanted to Know to Start, Grow, and Succeed in Your New Business

"Am I out of my $&*#@$ mind?"

"I'd better read this book!"

MICHAEL YASNY

Kingpin Publishing

So, You Want to Start Your Own Business

Everything You Ever Wanted to Know to Start, Grow, and Succeed in Your New Business
Michael Yasny
Kingpin Publishing

Published by Kingpin Publishing, Maple, Ontario, Canada
Copyright ©2022 Michael Yasny
All rights reserved.

Editor: Susan Crossman

Cover and Interior design: Davis Creative Publishing Partners, CreativePublishingPartners.com

Michael Yasny
So, You Want to Start Your Own Business: Everything You Ever Wanted to Know to Start, Grow, and Succeed in Your New Business
ISBN: 978-1-7782659-2-1 (hardback)
 978-1-7782659-1-4 (paperback)
 978-1-7782659-0-7 (ebook)

 2022

ATTENTION CORPORATIONS, UNIVERSITIES, COLLEGES AND PROFESSIONAL ORGANIZATIONS: Quantity discounts are available on bulk purchases of this book for educational, gift purposes, or as premiums for increasing magazine subscriptions or renewals. Special books or book excerpts can also be created to fit specific needs. For information, please contact Kingpin Publishing, michael@moneyconsultants.ca.

DEDICATION

The book is dedicated to my biggest fan my late father Malcolm Yasny. He provided me with unselfish devotion, kindness, love and encouragement. All the sacrifices he made for my welfare and the many comforts he provided me. He rejoiced in my achievements, guided me in my perplexities, and strengthened me in my trials and disappointments.

Everything I have learnt in life comes back to my father's encouragement to learn and never stop learning.

It is an honor to be known as Malcolm Yasny's son.

Table of Contents

FOREWORD   **1**

INTRODUCTION   **3**

CHAPTER 1 – Your Business Team:
Who Should Be on It?   **7**

    Your Lawyer 8

    Your Accountant................................ 11

    Your Business Broker........................... 12

    Your Broker Will Also: 14

CHAPTER 2 – How To Pick Your Team   **19**

    Choosing Your Lawyer 20

    Choosing Your Accountant..................... 22

    Choosing Your Business Broker................. 24

CHAPTER 3 – Your Partners and
Family Members   **31**

    Your Partners 31

    And What Makes a Good Silent Partner? 34

    What Makes a Good Partnership? 34

    Let's Look at These One at a Time. 36

CHAPTER 4 – How to Finance Your Business   41

Your Own Funds 45

Family and Friends (F&F) 46

Paying Interest on the Loan—and When to Start Paying Down the Principal............................ 49

Private Mortgages 52

Government Guaranteed Bank Loans.............. 54

CHAPTER 5 – What You Need to
Know About Factoring   57

Factoring, Also Known as Invoice Discounting or Receivable Financing........................... 57

What Do You Need to Know First? 57

Why is Factoring the Most Powerful Form of Financing Besides an Unlimited Line of Credit From a Bank? .. 65

The Most Frequent Questions People Ask About Factoring Are: 67

Here Are Some Important Details That Will Help Answer Those Questions: 67

Why Can't A Business Collect Funds and Forward the Money to Their Factoring Company?........... 72

And, Finally, What Will your Clients Think if You Are Using a Factoring Company?.............. 72

Factoring Versus Bank Financing 78

CHAPTER 6 – Purchase Order Financing and
Letters of Credit   83

Purchase Order Financing......................... 83

Purchase order financing is provided by 85

While We're Talking About POFs, Let's Take a Short Detour Into the World of Letters of Credit.......... 93

CHAPTER 7 – Leasing   97

Why Lease Your Equipment and
How Does Leasing Work? 97

Where Do You Get a Lease? 98

What Are the Rates for Leasing? Again,
It Depends on Various Factors, Such as: 100

CHAPTER 8 – Experience   113

Learning on the Job 113

Clearing Goods at Customs 118

Being Quick on Your Feet 121

Never Lower Your Price on the
Promise of More Business 122

Learn How to Cost 123

The Cost of Doing Business,
from a Mail Order Perspective 126

Dealing with Returns 128

Lesson Learned: No Returns. 129

Learning Your Business Lessons 130

CHAPTER 9 – Leaving Your Job   133

Ask About Entrepreneurial
Unemployment Insurance 134

Starting a Business That Competes with
Your Former Employer 137

Chapter 10 – Your Business Plan and Your Marketing Efforts   145

Do I Really Need a Business Plan?
The Answer is "Yes" and "No". 145

Marketing Your Business 146

CHAPTER 11 – Hiring, Delegating, and Being the President   153

How to Hire 153

Make Sure You Delegate 160

Being the President 161

Chapter 12 – Making Sales and Generating Profits   163

Sales 163

Creditworthiness 165

Insurance. 166

Your Credit Department 169

Understanding the Cost of
Your Product or Service 170

Here's What Goes into Your Costs: 170

What if Your Product or Service is Not Selling? 174

Perceived Value. 175

Bidding on Large Contracts is a
Good Way to Lose Money 176

A Story about Paint Can Lids 177

How Do You Get Your Product
into the Large Chains? 180

CHAPTER 13 – Are You an Inventor?   **183**
The Different Kinds of Inventors 183
Here's What I Witnessed at These Meetings: 184
Why Do People Invent Things? 185
Issues Around Patents 188
Do Your Market Research 190

CHAPTER 14 – What Could Possibly Go Wrong?   **195**
Structuring a Deal 195
Here Are Some Foreseeable Problems
You Might Face in Business: 197

CHAPTER 15 – What Else Could Go Wrong
...and Right?   **221**
Business v. the Pandemic 222
Personal Responsibility for Leases 225
Here's Another Situation You Might
Find Yourself In. 226

Summary Thoughts   **233**
Other Advice I Can Offer? 235

Appendix   **239**

Acknowledgements   **245**

About the Author   **247**

FOREWORD

Michael successfully powered his way through the situations recited in his book. His solutions are effective and if followed, will prove to be of great assistance to the reader.

Brian Morris LLP.

INTRODUCTION

Did you know that almost all business owners learn 80-90% of what they need to know about their business within the first year? And that it takes the rest of their business life to learn the remaining 10-20%? And did you know that 20% of new businesses fail within their first year? What's more, a whopping 30% fail in the second year, and 50% fail in year five. When you crunch all the numbers, 70% of new businesses don't make it to year ten.

In the business world, as in life, things are constantly changing, and we have to keep learning new things as we progress. Succeeding in a new business takes tenacity and a tough skin and still that's not enough. So, what makes you think you will be in the minority of those who succeed in their own business? Well, if you do things right from the beginning, you have a chance. You made your first lifechanging decision when you said "yes" to moving forward with your dream of starting your own business. Now that you're starting up, it's time to make the second even more important decision that will stack the odds in your favour: choosing the three key members of your team.

I will be mentioning your team members—your lawyer, your accountant, and your business broker—throughout this book to emphasize their importance in the success of your business. But meanwhile, I want to congratulate you and welcome you aboard the rollercoaster world of entrepreneurship. To own your own business is to say "yes" to a roller coaster ride of ups and downs, incredibly exciting and sometimes scary adventures, days that are exhausting and other days that can be exhilarating, financially strapping, and financially freeing.

There are few things more exciting than starting your own business and you have already passed one of the major requirements of being a successful business owner: you have acknowledged that there are many things you do not know about owning a business by purchasing this book. And I'll bet you want more of the ups, the excitement, the exhilaration, and the financial freedom than the stress and heartache that comes with being ill-prepared for the ride.

After decades on the inside edge of the success, failures, triumphs, and challenges of my own businesses—and those of my clients—I have become passionate about helping other people learn how to avoid the problems and misery that all too often comes along with being an entrepreneur. I've written this book to share a lot of information I wish I'd known when I was first starting out and I offer it up in the sincere wish that you, too, will come to appreciate the thrill and the wonder of running your own successful business.

Please read on knowing I am wishing you well and cheering you on. And let me know if you have questions that are not answered here. Who knows, this could be the first of several books on the topic. There's a lot to know about running your own business. And we all have to start somewhere. Which brings us to Chapter One…

– Michael Yasny

April 2022

CHAPTER 1

Your Business Team: Who Should Be on It?

Throughout the book you will find me talking about **Your Team**. I bring this up often because, quite frankly, a business idea and a business plan are nothing without the support of a dedicated team.

"What's a business team?" you ask. Well, before any business starts, it should have a three-member team in place.

And "who's on the team?" you ask? Well, you need a carefully chosen lawyer, an accountant, and a business broker or mentor. These are the professionals who are neither partner nor lender to your business, but the people you will go to for support and guidance. There is much more that your team can help you with as your business grows and so you want to be sure that they know what you're doing. A quick email or call once a month just to say, "hello," and to report on what has happened since you last spoke, is sufficient…supplemented by a commitment to discussing the details of every big decision with one or more of your team members *before* you make it.

If you do this, then you'll have the comfort of knowing that if your business ever gets into trouble, your team will be pretty much up to speed with your business and can act quickly to protect you. They also add a layer of professionalism to your business whenever you must deal with problems with your suppliers, customers, any licensing boards you belong to, and the government. They are also key partners if you are ever involved in any lawsuits.

Your team wants you to succeed, so let them help you succeed. Your lawyer should be a commercial lawyer, not your cousin the real estate lawyer. Your accountant should be an accountant who handles small businesses as a big part of their accounting practice. And the business broker should be a broker who arranges financing solutions from every alternative financing source.

These people are worth every cent you pay them, and they will save you countless dollars.

Here's what you need about how integral the team is for the success of your business:

YOUR LAWYER

The more your lawyer helps you from the start, the less it will cost to fix future problems later...and every business runs into problems. Your lawyer is the person you will go to in every situation that needs your signature; he or she will review every legal document involved, especially any documentation that requires your personal guarantee.

Absolutely every document is put before your lawyer for review. He or she will prepare or advise you on partnership agreements, financial documents, lease documents for your premises, etc. **You must provide your lawyer with every document no matter how simple it appears, before signing it.** This is just as important on day one of your business as it is 30 years later.

Please know that no matter what your lawyer charges for these reviews, it will be a fraction of the cost they will charge to get you out of trouble if you signed documents without their prior inspection. And having a lawyer behind you will show you are an entrepreneur who protectively surrounds themselves with professionals.

The first way to keep legal expenses down is to have the right lawyer reviewing all your business's documents. Did I mention that every document must be reviewed by your lawyer? Aside from keeping you out of trouble and showing how professional you are, insisting that your lawyer must review all business-related documents is a great way to prevent getting pressured into signing something you are leery of signing. If someone says you don't need your lawyer to review such a simple document, run, and run *quickly*. Honest businesspeople will never have a problem with you asking your lawyer to review their documents before signing.

Your lawyer will also incorporate your business. Yes, Incorporate. INCORPORATE, *INCORPORATE*, **INCORPORATE!** Did I say incorporate?! If you are not incorporated, all your personal assets are available to your creditors if something goes wrong. Incorporating your business is not expensive and will in most cases protect your personal assets. When choosing this member of your team, fees are secondary. I'm not suggesting that you need a $1,000 an hour lawyer to help you incorporate and protect your new business, but you do need a lawyer who has experience in the commercial business world. The right lawyer for your business could end up saving you a hundred times their fees, whereas a less expensive lawyer with no experience is not a good bet. Get references from other businesses, investigate potential lawyers with their governing body, and research them on the internet before you call them.

Another way to keep expenses down is to pay your lawyer on the same day they send you their invoice. Never let it become a 30-, 60-, or 90-day payable. The faster you pay the lawyer the more attentive to your file they are, and I promise you, your legal costs will always be less than the legal costs of businesses that pay their lawyer in 30, 60 or 90 days.

If you own a personal residence with your spouse, you should consider putting the residence in your spouse's name. This is one way to protect your equity in your home. This is something your lawyer does to make sure the transfer is done correctly. If the transfer is done for love and affection, and not for money, there may be a period when creditors could reverse the title transfer. If the transfer is done with a monetary implication it must be for fair market value. Speak with your lawyer to best understand this.

If you buy a new house after you start your business, it's smart to remember this is an opportunity for the new title to only be in your spouse's name. Again, you need to have your lawyer involved to make sure that the title in only your spouse's name cannot be challenged. You do not want a creditor to be able to attach your debt to your spouse, or to your property. Your lawyer will explain all the details of this so you understand what you can do to protect yourself.

YOUR ACCOUNTANT

Your accountant helps structure the financial wellbeing of your business, making sure your financial records are organized correctly from the day you open your business. He or she will help set up your financial records, help prepare or review your business plan, make sure you understand what's in the professional financial plan that you will present to potential lenders, and explain to you all the costs of doing business.

Your accountant will help write and/or review your business plan and make changes necessitated by your changing business. Your accountant is the person to whom you refer lenders considering taking on your business when they have questions about your business and financing.

If your accountant suggests that you stay a sole proprietor at the beginning to save money, he or she is not a business accountant, and therefore not the right accountant for you. Go find another accountant.

You don't want an accountant who is only available to you once a year when you need your financials prepared. You want your accountant to be a readily available financial business adviser, so keep him or her up to speed with your business. You'll appear professional to lenders and even to large buyers who need to understand your financial capabilities if they are going to forward financing or large orders.

Both your accountant and your lawyer should be kept up to speed with any changes to your business, such as larger or smaller sales periods, problems collecting on a large invoice, a lawsuit against you, tax arrears, the need to hire more general employees, or the need to fill a management position.

YOUR BUSINESS BROKER

The third member of your team is your business broker or business mentor. Your business broker is going to be there for every big decision your business makes, and this starts with helping you with your business's financing needs. He or she will help you stretch your limited financial resources when everyone has their hands out and are not willing to give your new business credit. He or she will make sure you have access to every business financing opportunity available to you. They will make sure that one financing opportunity does not prevent you from getting financing from other lenders. And they will help you deal with credit situations with your suppliers, as well as with your clients. Your business broker is the first person you will call regarding almost every aspect of your business. Have a question, need an answer? Call your broker—even before you seek help from your lawyer or accountant.

A good broker has a good understanding of the law, accounting, bankruptcy rules, business negotiating, and all the different alternative business financing options that are available. A good broker understands what the banks are looking for and will help you prepare your business so you can seek bank financing as soon as possible. He or she is every bit as important as your lawyer and accountant, if not more important. Your broker understands financing. He or she knows that the least costly financing option is not always the best financing option. He or she knows that your business will need different financing options for different aspects of your business. A lawyer will protect you when you sign a financial document, but they can rarely advise you on the correct financing option for your business, or how it might affect your ability to get different financing in the future.

YOUR BROKER WILL ALSO:

- Help you deal with your suppliers and help you understand why dealing with one supplier is better for you than another, even if that supplier is more expensive, is giving shorter payment terms, or both. Longer payment terms and less expensive supplies are not always in your business's best interest.

- Help you determine if you should extend credit, demand Cash on Demand (COD), or even suggest that you do not sell to a customer, even if they are going to pay COD. Bad clients are almost always a problem and never worth the trouble.

- Help you negotiate better terms with your lenders. The broker will have access to many different lenders in the same lending industries and will be able to help you lock in the best financing deal available.

- Help you structure tax arrears arrangements with the tax department and help you get financing from lenders that would have said "no" because they were worried about having the government seize the security they need to take to provide the financing.

Let's Elaborate:

When businesses come to me for factoring, I don't just take the client to any factoring company, or to the company with the best rates. I take them to the factoring company that specializes in their industry. I go to the factoring company looking for the arrangement that I would provide a client, which may not exactly be the same terms that factoring company might have offered if the client called the factoring company directly.

Since I know what the factoring companies are looking for, I can structure a deal that would be better for my client and still meet the factoring company's requirements.

Sometimes a financing deal is not exactly cookie cutter, and one must think outside the box to get it completed. The business owner is always at a disadvantage when dealing with lenders. The account managers (salespeople) for lenders are rarely thinking outside the box to get a deal done, and that is where an experienced broker can help turn a "no" into a "yes." Your broker will always be able to present a financing opportunity to a lender better than you, the owner, can and they will also know when to contact the person who makes the final credit decision if the deal actually does work, but the account manager does not see how it fits into the lender's structure.

One of the biggest worries a lender has when providing financing is around how the business stands today and will stand tomorrow with the tax department. The tax department can and often does interfere with the assets of a business, even if those assets have been given as security to a lender.

You never want to have to fight with the tax department, even if you are right and will eventually win. Remember, the tax department never goes out of business and will always be around. They have the time and money to fight and generally do not play fair. Unlike being charged with a crime, where it is up to the government to prove you are guilty, the tax department assumes you are guilty and acts accordingly.

You might think you should have your lawyer or even better your accountant make arrangements with the tax department, but I have never met a lawyer—and I'm pretty sure I have never met an accountant—who actually knows how to deal with the tax department regarding your arrears.

Here is an example of a tax situation that will stop you in your tracks when looking for financing, regardless of what financing you are looking at:

Company A has gotten behind with their tax remittances in the amount of $200,000. They have found a factoring company that wants to factor their $400,000 in invoices. During their due diligence the factoring company discovered the tax debt and are only prepared to finance the invoices if they can use the first $200,000 to pay the tax arrears. This makes sense: the factoring company is getting a client and can protect themselves against the government garnishing receivables that the factoring company has purchased.

Now, let's say the company owes $400,000 in tax remittances and only has $200,000 in receivables. Almost every single factoring company will say, "sorry *we can't help you until you have paid off your tax arrears." However, if that company used me as their broker, I would show the factoring company how they could purchase those receivables without any worry about the tax department garnishing the receivables. That is why you have a business broker as part of your team.*

Your team is there to protect you and help you succeed beyond your dreams. Pick the right team members and you will never be alone. Don't think you need a team at the beginning? Then be prepared to spend a lot more of your time and money on everything that comes your way.

*The old saying, **"an ounce of prevention is worth a pound of cure"** is certainly true when it comes to your team.*

CHAPTER 2

HOW TO
PICK YOUR TEAM

Now that we know who needs to be on your team, and why, let's explore how you go about ensuring you select the absolute best people for each job. My first advice is to do the same as you would when looking to hire employees: ask people you know, like, and trust for recommendations. Prospective members of your team could be professionals you have crossed paths with in the past. For example, I went up against a lawyer in court more than once and I'd hire him without question. Even though he did not work for me I still noticed how good he was.

Set up an appointment with the professional for an interview. Let them know you're looking for them to join your team. The right individual will be willing to meet for at least one hour for free although I'm not sure you will need a full hour. Move on from anyone who says they can only give you 15 minutes for free. Getting an unpaid hour with them is your first test.

CHOOSING YOUR LAWYER

You want a lawyer with commercial experience and litigation experience doesn't hurt but is not necessary as long as someone in your lawyer's firm does have it. You don't want a large downtown firm, nor do you want a one-person firm, and it would be ideal if the firm is geographically close, although that's not mandatory. Give the lawyer a brief outline of your business and tell them you are putting a three-person team in place. You are looking for an out-of-office corporate lawyer who is available when needed. You will be passing every document that will require your signature corporately and/or personally past them for review. Ask if they have any experience in your industry. Although this is not a dealbreaker, it certainly would be a benefit.

Get to know the lawyer personally during the interview. Talk about everything: family, sports, other interests. Build some rapport, see that you share values, that you like each other as people, aside from the business relationship you are about to embark on. If you do not like the lawyer, do not hire the lawyer because I guarantee you will not have regular communications with someone you do not like. If you do not get along with the lawyer, how likely is it that the other members of your team will like the lawyer? You are building your business team and it's best when you can all work easily together. There will be disagreements from time to time within your team but if you all respect each other, things will work out. You're the captain of the team, you get to make final decisions, so take charge.

Be upfront and clear with your lawyer that when you call, you want them to pick up and if they can't, you expect a return call ASAP. You do not need to be a large client to make this arrangement with the lawyer, but you need to have it. You can't nor should you have to wait days to get a call back even for a simple question. Here's what you will offer your lawyer to agree to your request: you will pay his or her bill the day you get it. You will be the only client who does this, and your lawyer will want to make sure you are happy and continue to pay the bill immediately. Waiting 30 days to pay the bill won't save you money, but you will save a great deal by paying the bill immediately. You can't demand more from your lawyer if you do not provide them with a reason to want to meet your request. I know from personal experience that paying your bill will achieve your goal of ensuring your lawyer pays more attention to you as a client, regardless of the size client you are. Rarely, if ever, will you be charged for every little call or review.

You will not hide legal problems until they become a huge problem. This just makes your lawyer's job harder, more time consuming and less likely to be successful, not to mention, more expensive. Again, I must stress that you pay your lawyer's invoices right away otherwise… what leg do you have to stand on in expecting immediate, easy access to him or her?

No matter the industry, the best service is always given to the person or business who pays their bill the fastest and with no complications.

To Elaborate:

I've only had two different lawyers during my business career. I worked well with them, and they worked well with me because everyone respected and followed a couple of major rules: they pick up the phone when I call, and I pay their invoices immediately. When this arrangement stops working, look for a different lawyer.

I replaced my first lawyer after about five years. I always paid the bill, the lawyer always called me back, and we never lost a case. But when the trust between us was broken, it was time to find a new lawyer. Sometimes a supplier forgets who the client is and when that happens, it's time to find another supplier.

I have used my current lawyer for the past 20 years, and nothing has given me reason to believe we will not continue to work well together for the next 20 years (except if one of us retires).

CHOOSING YOUR ACCOUNTANT

You want to find the right accountant for your business in pretty much the same way you look for your lawyer and business broker. You want an accountant who works with small- and medium-sized businesses and who also has experience in the industry in which your business operates. You don't need a top-four accounting firm, but you do need one large enough to be experienced in providing review engagements and audited financial statements for when your business becomes successful enough to warrant them. Your accountant should also be experienced in preparing financial packages for lenders. You want to have contact with your accountant every month and every quarter, not just annually. The communication can be direct with you or through your bookkeeper. Either way, your accountant will want to make sure your bookkeeping system fits into the system the accountant uses.

The more professionals surrounding your business, the more professional your business will look. Perhaps your new lawyer could recommend an accounting firm, or your accounting firm might recommend a lawyer for your team. In most cases the referral will help satisfy the need for your lawyer and accountant to know each other and work together to help your business succeed.

If you pay your accountant immediately, you will be the only client they have who does. No one pays their accountant immediately except those who are asked to pay up front. Your accountant will go out of their way to help their only immediate payer.

CHOOSING YOUR BUSINESS BROKER

Without question, the right broker is the hardest member of the team to find. Very few brokers will even understand the idea of being part of your team. And although I might be biased, I think the broker is the most important team member. Very few brokers have the knowledge and experience—as well as the vision and creative thinking—to provide guidance in every alternative financing space. They'll say they have *contacts* in every alternative financing space, but what you really want is for them to have *direct knowledge about* each of these specialty finance areas.

When you interview a prospective business broker, don't just ask them which different financings they handle; ask them to explain each one to make sure they understand each one themselves, even if you don't. You will be able to tell if they really do understand these different financings just by how they describe them.

Here is a guide to the types of questions you want to ask potential brokers before deciding on one. I've also included the answers you should hear from them.

1. How long have you been providing alternative financing?

    I would say five-plus years should be the minimum. You want someone who is making a living at it and anyone who has been doing it for at least five years is making a living.

2. What were you doing before getting into alternative financing?

    A great answer would be something like, "Running my own B2B company or working in the commercial department of a bank."

3. What is your financial background/what area of financing did you start in?

    A good answer would be, "Working in any of the alternative businesses—factoring, leasing, buying and selling businesses, etc." Banking would also be a good one. This might sound strange, but a bookkeeper would be a good background and being an accountant would not. Only an accountant who had a problem would leave accounting to work in a business field that generates mostly a commission income. Bookkeepers see all the problems with small- and medium-sized businesses, so they would really understand the great need business have for alternative financing.

4. Have you ever had your own business before getting into the financing business?

    "Yes," is a really good answer.

5. What was that business and what happened to it?

    It doesn't really matter what business you were in but a B2B is much better than a B2C. A person who had a business that failed because of cash flow problems is a person with firsthand knowledge of what happens to businesses that need financing and can't find it. This is the kind of person I looked for when I was hiring a salesperson for a factoring company.

6. What are the different financing arrangements you can help my business with?

You don't want to hear "I can help you with all kinds of different financings." That's not specific enough. You want to hear the actual kinds of financing they can help you with, such as factoring, purchase order financing, leasing, government-backed loans, and, hopefully, more.

7. What is the largest financing you have arranged and what kind of financing was it?

I would say somewhere in the $500,000 + area is a good answer. This could be a one-time financing or several financings for one company that added up over $500,000 over several years.

8. How do you charge for your services?

Charging should be a combination of the lender paying the broker—as in factoring—and adding a fee to the deal—as in leasing and private mortgage arrangements. Another positive response would be adding a small upfront fee, say, on a government deal, with the balance payable on the successful conclusion of a deal. A broker who earns most of their fees on success is a broker you want on your team. You may at times go to your broker for help with non-financing situations, at which point the broker will become a consultant and probably charge you an hourly fee.

9. Do you provide any of the financing yourself or do you just arrange financing through lenders?

   This is just a question to see if the broker lends their own money in certain situations and the answer will most likely be that they do, but only on private mortgages. It's really not that important and it's very doubtful they do.

10. Do you ever get involved with bankruptcy situations, tax arrears, litigation?

    Since a businessowner is going to contact their broker first before going to the lawyer or accountant in a situation like bankruptcy or litigation over tax arrears, you want to know they have a pretty good understanding of these areas. The broker is the one who will come up with a plan for the lawyer and/or accountant to execute—or should be the one with a plan.

11. Have you ever been involved with helping a client buy a business?

    I would hope the broker has been involved in the purchasing or selling of a business in the past. This is not really mandatory, but you never know when you might want to sell or buy a business and your broker is—or should be—the first person on your team you discuss this with.

12. If your client asks, do you have a commercial lawyer and/or small business accountant you would be confident recommending?

    You really want a broker who has connections in the legal and accounting world. This is not a dealbreaker because everyone knows lawyers and accountants. But do the lawyers and accountants know the broker well? Ask for some referrals under the pretence of including them on your team. If there is a good relationship, you will get a few names and you can call the referrals to get a better idea of the respect they have for the broker.

13. Do you have any direct experience in arranging government grants and loans?

The answer should be, "yes." Everyone should have a contact list of associates who specialize in grants and government-backed loans. It's not necessary for the broker to be an expert, you just want them to know who the experts are.

14. Have you ever helped any of your clients with letters of credit and standby letters of credit?

This is a specialized area, sometimes used in conjunction with purchase order financing. The answer hopefully will be, "yes," and not, "you get letters of credits from a bank." Letters of credit and standby letters of credit are great financing tools and need to be understood well. It's better to hear, "No," than "sure I can help with letters of credit." If they say yes to being able to help, ask them to tell you about some they have arranged and test them on their knowledge of standby letters of credit.

Even though your lawyer, accountant, and broker are part of your team—*especially* since they are—you should always show your appreciation for them by referring new business to them.

When trouble finds your business—and eventually it will:

No matter how small or big, how new, or old, every business eventually finds itself with a problem. Whether it's financial or not to begin with, that problem will always turn into a financial problem.

CHAPTER 3

Your Partners and Family Members

People often go into a business with one or more partners because either they can't raise the capital required to keep the business afloat or they don't have the knowledge or experience they feel they need to generate success. There are a lot of issues around this that will affect the success or failure of your business. Family considerations are also part of the success equation. So, here's what you need to know:

YOUR PARTNERS

Partnership is usually related to financing. They are made up of two or more people and there are two simple categories of partners:

1. A working partner.
2. A silent partner.

A working partner is just that: someone who works in the business alongside you. They are not necessarily an equal partner (they would have more, less, or equal ownership with you) but they work in and own part of the business with you. Generally, all partners bring money to the business and the amounts usually determine the percentage of their ownership of the business. However, there are some working partners who bring more than just money. They might have years of experience, important connections, or the product (invention) itself.

A silent partner is just an investor. In my experience, a silent partner is always the money partner. They're not involved in the day-to-day running of the business, and they don't work in the business. Silent partners are, in many cases, a sounding board for the working partner to help them navigate changes in the business. Usually, the silent partner has a tremendous amount of experience in business and will serve as a mentor when called upon.

However, the wrong silent partner **will become**—not *might* become—a serious problem for the business. **So, what makes for the *wrong* silent partner?**

1. The Micromanaging Type

   This is a partner who demands to be involved in every big and little decision you need to make. Such as:

   - Who are you going to hire for management positions?

   - Who's your lawyer going to be? Who will your accountant be?

   - How are you pricing your product or service?

This type gets involved in almost every decision that the person running the business should make.

2. The Unreliable Type

    This is the kind of partner you can't count on to come to the table and help financially in crisis time. Crisis time is not necessarily when things are going wrong, sometimes it's when everything is going too well, and more money is needed to keep the operation running smoothly. When I say, "can't count on," it's not because they do not have more money, but they want more of the company or a higher return to advance more funds, or they might even want you to hire one of their relatives before they provide the extra financing.

3. The Worst Type

    These people take advantage of a tight situation by demanding repayment of any loans they have advanced or by pulling any guarantees they have made to provide outside financing to the business. This is something a partner looking for more of the business does to force you to accept terms that are not in your best interest, with the alternative being that you will lose the business.

4. The Unwelcome Type

    This kind of partner shows up to the business unannounced, tells employees what to do and how do it and asks them questions about the business that should only be discussed with you, or at least with you present.

AND WHAT MAKES A GOOD SILENT PARTNER?

1. They Have Experience. But not necessarily in the business you are going to partner in.

2. They Know Money. Not only are they going to invest in your company, but they understand business financing.

3. You Can Count on Them. They are open to providing more financing directly or by arrangement if the business needs it without changing the makeup of the business ownership.

4. They Are Trusting. You agree together on who the business's lawyer and accountant should be.

5. They Are Approachable. And always, without condition, available as a sounding board for anything to do with the business.

6. They Are Precise. They want a partnership agreement that spells out everything that could come up in a partnership and which will protect both partners, not just them.

WHAT MAKES A GOOD PARTNERSHIP?

1. Little Overlap = Fewer arguments

   One of my first lessons about silent partnering was, "don't have a partner who does the same things as you do." And so, one person is the salesperson and the other runs the factory. One's the chef and the other runs the front of the restaurant.

2. A Partnership Agreement

   It's much easier to have an agreement before you start the business than to have to put one in place after the business encounters its first problem.

WHAT SHOULD BE IN YOUR PARTNERSHIP AGREEMENT?

a.) Who the lawyer for the company will be

b.) Who the accountant be for the company will be

c.) A shotgun clause

d.) What will happen if a further investment is needed, and one partner cannot provide more money

e.) A commitment from each partner to carry life insurance

f.) A succession agreement

g.) Pledging shares for personal reasons

h.) A commitment to give one owner the first right of refusal to an outside buyer

i.) A list of each partner's duties

j.) Whatever other conditions each partner and/or their lawyer may wish to include

LET'S LOOK AT THESE ONE AT A TIME.

The Lawyer and Accountant for the Company

The partnership agreement should cover all factors that relate to each partner's responsibilities, and it starts with each partner having **their own lawyer and accountant** to help with the writing of the partnership agreement. This way the professionals who are representing you have only your best interest to worry about.

The Shotgun Agreement

This ensures that if one partner is financially stronger than the other, then they cannot take advantage of the financially weaker partner by offering an unfairly low offer: the shotgun clause gives the weaker partner the right to buy the business at that price. A shotgun clause keeps things neat if one party wants to buy the other out. There are no negotiations, and the offer cannot be pulled. Your lawyer will be able to fully explain all aspects of the shotgun agreement.

Further Financing

Most businesses will need **more financing.** An agreement between partners must stipulate what the business is offering the partner who is reinvesting.

Life Insurance

The business needs to pay for life insurance on each partner. If one partner dies, then that partner's estate (wife or children) becomes a partner in the business. The estate might want to sell their shares and if the surviving partner does not have the resources to pay for the shares, those shares—or even the business itself—could be put up for sale. If both partners have life insurance, then it can be used to buy out the shares of the partner who dies. As the business grows in value, the life insurance should be increased.

Succession

Partners need to decide who will be allowed to succeed the partner who retires or dies. Not every partner wants to be partners with their partner's family, so the succession clause will spell out who is or isn't allowed to replace that partner. There can also be a clause stipulating that no family members are allowed to work for the company or have any ownership. Again, a discussion about that needs to take place at the beginning of the partnership.

Pledging Shares for Personal Reasons

As the business grows the value of the shares grow. One partner may need personal financing and their shares in the business are an asset. Should you allow those shares to be pledged to an outside lender? I say NO. The reason is that if the security (the shares) is called upon, the business could be forced to be sold, or the lender might become the new partner. Pledging of shares should only be available for the financing needs of the business.

First Right of Refusal

If the partners are approached by a buyer to purchase the business and one partner does not wish to sell, they should have the first right of refusal and be able to purchase the other partner's shares for the same price offered by the outside purchaser.

List of Duties

The partnership agreement should provide an agreed upon list of duties for each partner as well as a shared list of responsibilities for all partners.

Other Items

Other issues will arise that relate to the nature of the business that each partner's lawyer will want in the agreement. As well, each of the items above will be discussed and written into the agreement in much greater detail.

LET'S TALK ABOUT YOUR FAMILY

You may ask why I have listed family as a discussion point in this book. This is because your family members are always a big part of your decision to go into business for yourself. Family is where you get moral support, potential financing, partnership, and guidance, and yours are very important to the success of your business.

Whether it is your immediate family (spouse and children) or your parents and siblings, their support will become a big part of your success or failure. Are they with you on this? If not, you are going to meet with added pressure, which is more likely to contribute to the failure of your business than its success. You are asking your family to give up a lot for your dream of owning a business. They are giving up the security of you having a job and the consistent income it provides. They are giving up family time as you will be working more hours and days than you do as an employee. This might not be just for a few months or a year it could be for many years, depending on the business you start. I have never met a new business owner who stays within the 9-5, five-days-a-week structure.

Your new business will likely keep you from attending many family events because you must work, and your family members need to understand this before you start your business. If you need any family members to help in the business, are they willing to do so, and for how long? And what financial pressure are you putting on your family starting your new business?

- Are you using your home as security for financing?
- Are you asking your spouse to allow a second mortgage on your home?
- Will you have to sell your house?
- Or borrow money from retirement accounts?

These are just some of the pressures you are asking your family to take on for your dream. If your spouse is not 100% behind you and your business has the smallest hiccup, this will affect your relationship. I have mentioned needing your spouse's support for your new business's financing needs, but what if you are going to other family members? Are they willing to support you? What are you going to have to guarantee them for their financial support?

When taking on a family member as a partner, just like any partnership, the same agreements that were raised in the partnership section of this book will apply to you and your family partner. Even more so because you are adding a new and unfamiliar dimension to the familial relationship. Saying you are family so you don't need agreements will lead to problems you may never resolve.

The one good thing about having your family around—even if they are not working in the business—is there will be no shortage of insight, suggestions, and guidance coming your way for free.

These are pressures you need to know are part of starting a business when you have family member(s) involved. These pressures are on top of the normal pressures of starting a new business. There's nothing wrong with pressure—it helps many people succeed—but it also takes a toll and causes others to fail. So, the question is, are you a person who can handle this kind of pressure? Because it goes with starting a new business and never really disappears.

CHAPTER 4

How to Finance Your Business

Ask any business owner how much time they spend on finances and worrying about money, and I bet you're going to get pretty much the same answer. Whether they are just starting out, already enjoying success, or have failed at it, most will report they spend 50% or more of their time on this aspect of their business. Or at least until they figure it out. If you're spending 50% or more of your time worrying about money well, that's 50% or more of your time that you are not running and growing your business. So, again, financing is the most important part of your business, without which it does not matter how good your product or service is because you will not be able to deliver it.

This chapter will explain in detail some of the many different forms of financing a business can attract to finance their venture.

Let's start with everyone's favorite, **the Bank.**

First and foremost, the Bank is not interested in your new business and will not be providing you with any financing unless you can answer one question. That question is "What security do you have for the financing you wish the bank to provide to your business?" If you have hard security such as your wealth, the equity in your home, or someone will sign for a line of credit for your business, head straight to your bank.

However, if you don't have hard security—and the bank does not consider a large purchase order from a big box store, a billion-dollar company, or the government to be hard security—then all you need from your bank is a new business account. It's best to set that new business account up at a commercial/business branch rather than a local branch, as this is where you will go to look for bank financing down the road. It will be easier for the bank to watch your progress this way, and it means bank staff will be in a much better position to finance your business in the future.

When you're up and running, go introduce yourself and your business to the bank manager. This is not to ask for financing now that you are up and running. This is just to let them know you are in business and to tell them what that business is. You can ask what the bank's criteria are for giving your business a loan or line of credit without hard security. This way you and your accountant can start organizing your business for future bank financing right from the start of your business. Generally speaking, you will need at least two years of positive financial statements.

Take This Lesson from Me

You have heard this many times: a person buys a product from a company or a store and then reverse engineers it only to sell it back to the company for half the price they had been paying their original supplier. That is exactly what I did. One winter I noticed everyone was wearing fake fur earmuffs and I wondered why no one was wearing real fur earmuffs. So, I went to the fur department of a large department store and found they were selling real fur earmuffs. I bought a pair, had someone copy them for me in a few different furs and then went back and sold the earmuffs to the department store for half the price they were paying their current supplier.

Now, I needed money, not just for the furs and labor, but for the key to the earmuff business, the actual earmuff frame (which was a complete surprise to me). I had to order the frames from an importer which required me to execute a letter of credit. So, I went to my father for advice, and he suggested I contact his friend at the bank. The next day I made an appointment to meet with the bank manager. I got dressed up, took my purchase order from the department store, and met with the bank manager. After the pleasantries, he asked how he could help me.

I explained, "I have a large order from a department store, and I have also made arrangements to sell my new product at a retail mall, so I would like to set-up a line of credit for $25,000 please."

The bank manager asked, "Okay, how would you like to secure the loan?"

"I have a purchase order from the department store which I can use for the security, and I will also be selling my product from a retail outlet," I said.

"What else do you have as security for the line of credit?" the bank manager asked.

That threw me off guard.

"I have nothing else—why, are the purchase order and retail operation not sufficient?"

The manager told me that, "the purchase order and retail store are not good enough security for the line of credit. How do I know you will deliver, or that anyone will buy your products? Therefore, the bank needs security that will cover the line of credit in the event you cannot."

*This was my first lesson in financing: no security, no financing. In this case my father signed for the line of credit, and I was in business. Unfortunately, not everyone starting a business has hard security or access to someone with the necessary security that would encourage a bank to finance their new business. There are other options for a new business to acquire the financing they need to start their new business and we'll discuss several of them in detail. *

YOUR OWN FUNDS

This is exactly what it sounds like. You use your own money to fund your business. This is the easiest funding to use (when it is available). No one can tell you what you can or cannot use the funds for. You do not need to sign any documents or pledge any security for the funds. The one problem with using your own funds without a backup financing plan in place, is that you might run out of your own money before you are able launch or get your business to the next stage. Now you are at the mercy of other lenders who might take advantage of your predicament.

So, before you use all your own money, have a backup financing plan in place. Having your team in place before you start your business will help you with your backup plan. As I mentioned earlier, your team is made up of three outside professionals: your lawyer to protect your rights, your accountant to bring a financing plan to your business, and a business broker to help with your financing needs today and tomorrow. We will discuss the roles of your team members in much greater detail throughout the book but for now, suffice to say that a business without all the players in place is more challenged to succeed.

When you fund your business with your own money, this is known as a **shareholder loan**. You should register security on your business (through a UCC1 or a GSA — your lawyer will explain what these documents are) and include the payment terms and interest rate.

Now you are secured creditor. You can always post-pone your security position to other lenders and remain a secured creditor down the road if that is advantageous to you. Even if you are charging interest to your business, and for some reason you cannot afford the interest payment, postpone it—you control the loan. The interest rate you charge and pay back to yourself is taxable, so speak with your team accountant on the interest rate you want to charge yourself.

This is where your team comes together to help you with your self-funding set-up. Your lawyer will register the security and the accountant will determine what is in the best interest for you and the business with regards to the interest rate you are going to charge your business. The best thing to do is to try and hold some of or all your money in reserve. Try using other lenders' funds (called OPM—Other People's Money) before your own. You might need some of your funds to attract other lenders to provide financing to you, so having your own funds in reserve is helpful.

FAMILY AND FRIENDS (F&F)

This is a great place to go for financing, but it comes with a unique set of challenges. First, you must sell your F&F on your idea. Then you must discuss how much money you will need. Are you going to pay interest or give them part of your business in exchange for the loan? When are you going to pay them back and what happens if you can't do that when you said you would?

What if you need more money in order to keep the business open and they do not have the ability to give you more—or worse, they won't? How do you approach them to sell them on your idea? How much money do you ask for, do you take it all at once or in stages, do you pay interest and, if so, how much? Do you give them an ownership position in your business? Do you give them security on your business? Do you let them work for you as a condition of the loan?

This is how I would start. Since no one keeps their new business idea a secret, your F&F likely already know about your plans for business. Arrange for one meeting with everyone who's shown interest in your business. Provide them with a professional business plan before the meeting. Have your team (lawyer, accountant, and business broker) present to show how professional and organized you are.

At the meeting be prepared for every possible question that can come up and every if/and/but excuse they will throw at you because they are going to come at you, and fast.

Now the time comes for you to ask for what you need. I've seen too many borrowers ask for less than they need, hoping that they'll have a better chance at getting the loan (and people do this even when they go to a bank). This is one of the biggest financing mistakes not just new business owners make, but most. Always ask for more than you think you will need. This is because nothing in business works according to plan. It takes longer to get up and running and to make sales; suppliers all have their hands out because they do not want to issue credit to a new business or, if you are lucky enough to get some credit, they will be holding you to very tight credit limits and payment terms. If you were able to secure some credit terms you need to make sure you keep them, especially when you are just starting your business.

It is very difficult to go back to your lenders and explain that you need more money. Therefore, I suggest you ask for at least 50% more than you believe you will need. Paying the extra back sooner is a lot easier than asking for another loan from your lenders. They are going to give you the third degree before they even entertain advancing you more money. They will lose confidence in you and your business if you must go back to them for more money. And they might ask for security, an ownership stake in your business, higher interest if they were charging interest, or a larger percentage than they requested for the first loan.

I would suggest you take all the money at once. This way you never have to ask for it, wondering or hoping it's still available. There's nothing worse than going to get the next tranche of funds only to find out that your lender has put the money to work somewhere else. If it makes you feel better about it, call the extra interest on the extra money insurance.

Is it better to pay interest or give up shares in a new business? I recommend paying interest, except in one scenario: when you do not have to pay back the loan if the business fails because the lender's funding was an investment, not a loan. This is unlikely to happen in a new business, but it never hurts to ask.

PAYING INTEREST ON THE LOAN—AND WHEN TO START PAYING DOWN THE PRINCIPAL

Interest should be based on percentage points over prime and should change either every time the prime goes down or up, or once a year on the anniversary of the loan. A fair interest rate would be between 4-6% over prime, but some lenders will want a fixed interest rate—probably in the 8-12% range.

You want to pay interest for as long as you can. I would suggest you try and negotiate interest only for at least two years before you start paying back principal. The first two years are the most critical for your business and you do not want to be pressured to pay back the principal that your business desperately needs for cash flow. When you do start to pay back the principal, it should be paid back over a specific time period, and not in one or several lump sum payments. Cash is king and the longer you can stretch out the principal payments the better your business will run.

Remember: once you start paying back the principle, it's highly unlikely you'll be able to go back and reborrow the money, which is why I don't think you should pay the principle back early or start paying it back before two years has passed. The longer you can just be in an interest-only payment position with your lenders, the better your business's cash position will be. Another reason to try and wait at least two years before paying back the principle is that you will then have two years of financials completed. Once you have two years of financials, you are in a position—if you are making money—to go to a bank for financing. Generally, banks will not look at businesses that have not been in operation for at least two years *unless they have hard security*.

Whatever the terms of the loan are, make sure you have the right to pay it back at any time before the due date. You should also have the right to make partial payments towards the principal. I'm not suggesting you do that, just that the option should be there for you.

If you are paying a fair interest return to your lenders, many will be content to just keep collecting the interest and they will be happy to let the principal sit on your books.

You will probably be asked to sign a promissory note recognizing the loan. This can be in the form of a promissory note guaranteed by you and/or your company or it could be a Uniform Commercial Code 1 (UCC1 in the US) or a General Security Agreement (GSA in Canada) against your company. Both are basically personal guarantees from your company. It's much better to sign these security agreements rather than a personal guarantee but you are not able to really negotiate the security, so sign what you must in order to get the financing to start and run your business. However, never sign before your lawyer, accountant, and business broker have reviewed the deal and given their professional opinions.

Do your best not to sign a **demand loan.** You never want to be in a position where your lender, for whatever reason, demands repayment of the loan (that being said, bank loans are almost always demand loans). The timing will never be good and could jeopardize your business and relationships with other lenders if they get wind of the demand and you are not able to pay back the loan. This is where your team comes in again: the lawyer to protect you regarding the legal documents, the accountant to budget the interest and principal, and the broker to negotiate the repayment terms.

No matter what, make sure your interest payments are made on time. If you pay by check, send postdated checks, if you pay by e-transfer, make sure that payment is made on the interest date—and if that date falls on a weekend or a holiday, send it early, if possible, or at least make sure it arrives on the morning of the first day the banks are open. Lenders get nervous when the interest check does not come on time. When it comes on time every time, they don't often ask many questions about your business. Also, paying on time may lead to unsolicited calls to see if you need more money. Lenders like interest paid on time and do not like working to collect. Provide them with that scenario and your business will have one less problem.

By the way, providing a job for someone as a condition for receiving a loan is not something you want to entertain. Nothing good can come from that. If you end up having to let that person go, you're going to find your relationship with your lender very strained, especially when it's a family member or friend. Getting money from F&F is generally easier than anywhere else in the short term but in the long term it can put a lot of stress on you, your family or friends, and your business.

PRIVATE MORTGAGES

A private mortgage is a mortgage that is given by either a private mortgage company or a private individual. Unlike a mortgage from a bank, where the borrower and the property must meet certain lending criteria, a private mortgage is based almost always on the equity in the property and not on the borrower's ability to pay back the loan. Most private mortgages are interest only, which is exactly what you want.

Private mortgage terms generally extend one year but can sometimes go for two years. At the end of one year, you can either pay back the mortgage, pay part of it and renew, or just renew—as long as the lender is agreeable, which they generally will be, if the interest payments have been paid on time with no problems. A private mortgage is an easy way to raise funds for your business (except for the fact that you need your spouse's support—not something that is always easy to get). You can use the funds for your business without restrictions from your lender.

When arranging a mortgage on your property to be used for your business, I would suggest that you document the loan from you personally to your business. I would also charge your business at least 1% more than the second mortgage lender is charging you. Show the loan as a real loan to your business, earning interest. I would also register a security charge against your business for the loan. Your business pays you and you pay the mortgagor. Speak to your lawyer about the security registration and your accountant about the interest rate.

You may be asking yourself why you wouldn't go to a bank for a second mortgage or use the equity in your home to secure a line of credit and that is a great question. The answer is that I assume you already did that, and you were turned down. In order to go to the bank for a second mortgage or line of credit, you must personally qualify for the loan, which you might not be able to do. If you do qualify for a larger mortgage from the bank, ask if the bank will provide you with a line of credit using your house as security for the business line of credit. That would be the best scenario. If you need more money than they are offering in the form of a secured line of credit, then you might be able to get a higher advance with a new first mortgage. But before you take the new first mortgage, ask the bank if they're going to charge a penalty for breaking the existing mortgage. Now, take the information on a new first with the bank, the conditions of a line of credit, and the expenses of a private mortgage straight to your accountant to help you make the right financial decision for you and your business. The lower cost financing is not always the best financing for your business.

Getting a private mortgage, although much more expensive, is much easier and only involves the equity in your home. Unlike loans from Family and Friends—who will be reluctant to advance more funds if you need more money—the mortgage lender or a new lender would be happy, no questions asked, to advance you more money on two conditions:

1. All interest payments have been made on time during the past year.
2. There is enough equity in your property to support a larger mortgage.

The private mortgage is easy, quick, short-term financing for your business and your business makes all the payments.

GOVERNMENT GUARANTEED BANK LOANS

Both the United States and Canada offer government guaranteed loans to small businesses. In the US, loans are provided through the Small Business Administration (SBA), and it is administered by approved lenders. The limits are much greater than in Canada, with loans going up to $5,000,000. Each loan has several qualifications you must meet with regards to what you can or cannot spend the money on, how much you must guarantee, and what kind of business the loan will go to support.

In Canada, the loan is known as the Canadian Small Business Loan (CSBL), and it is administered by the major Canadian banks. Loans are limited to $350,000 for businesses themselves, and $1,000,000 for the purchase of real estate for your business. Each loan will have several qualifications you must meet with regards to what you can or cannot spend the money on, how much you must guarantee, and what kind of business the loan will go to support.

It's best to read up on the qualifications of each loan you are looking for. If you do not qualify now, do your best to understand what you need to do to put your business in a position to qualify for the loan in the future. You do not need to be a brand-new business to apply for these loans.

The best suggestion I have for you with this financing is to find a company that helps you apply at the institutions that provide these government backed loans. They are worth every dollar they are going to charge you. Most will only charge if they're successful in arranging the loan for you. The fee on success can be up to 10% of the amount arranged but that will go down as the loan amount goes up. Some companies may levy a small charge to cover the cost of putting together a business plan and your application.

You shouldn't pay more for the business plan than whatever the average cost that business plan preparers charge in your area. Please let them prepare the business plan (even if you already have one), as they know exactly how the lender wants it to be prepared.

If they do not think you will qualify, they will not spend their time putting the application in. On the other hand, if they feel you'll have a greater chance of getting approved for the loan in the future, they'll help you set up your business in a way that maximizes your chances of getting approved. Try not to apply for financing unless you're 90% sure you will be approved. If you put in an application before you're ready and you're refused, it could be a year or more before you can put in another application to that lender.

* * * * *

These financing opportunities are great, and they each have an important role to play in the financing of a business. But did you know there are other options available? For example, a lot of people don't know it, but *factoring* is another powerful tool your business can use to manage cashflow and expand your opportunities. Turn the page to find out more about it!

CHAPTER 5

What You Need to Know About Factoring

FACTORING, ALSO KNOWN AS INVOICE DISCOUNTING OR RECEIVABLE FINANCING

Originally, factoring used to be the insuring of a business's receivables, not the selling of them. Somehow over the years it has changed to mean the selling of creditworthy receivables to a factoring company.

Other than when an unlimited line of credit is available from a bank, factoring is the most powerful form of financing a growing B2B company can have. Since few businesses qualify for lines of credit that far exceed their needs, factoring is the way to go; it's the financing option that is going to solve all your business's growing financing needs.

WHAT DO YOU NEED TO KNOW FIRST?

1. You must be incorporated for at least one day. That's right, your business does not have to be up and running for any specific period because unlike

a bank loan or line of credit, a factoring company is not lending you money, they are buying your finished invoices.

2. You must have invoices that have been delivered to other businesses, not to members of the public.

3. You need creditworthy clients, or the ability to sell to them.

4. What does creditworthy mean? Any corporations that the factoring company is prepared to give credit to. Generally, this means corporations that have revenues of $100,000,000-plus, and that are making a profit.

5. There Are Minimums. The average size of your invoices and your monthly gross average needs to meet the minimum volume that the factoring company is looking for. Each factoring company will have their own minimums. The smallest now is about an average of $1,000 per invoice and about $25,000 -$50,000 a month in creditworthy receivables. However, most factoring companies are looking for double those numbers. This doesn't mean they won't take on small companies with creditworthy payers if they believe your business can grow to meet their minimum numbers sooner rather than later.

6. Industry Specifics. Your industry must be one that the factoring company finances. Every factoring company will choose industries that they will and won't factor. So, depending on your industry you might have to search until you find the one that

factors your industry. Your business broker will know all the factoring companies that service your industry.

7. Security Documents. You will be asked to sign a security document giving the factoring company security on your receivables and probably a first-place charge on all other assets as well. At the very least the security will be a first-place charge on your receivables and a second-place charge on all other assets. If the factoring company factors with recourse—meaning if something goes wrong you will still owe them the money—they'll probably ask you to sign a personal guarantee.

You might ask, "why do I need to personally guarantee creditworthy payers such as governments, banks, and big box stores? The answer is that the only thing that can go wrong is that your company does not fulfil its obligations to your client. So, really there is nothing to guarantee if you stand behind your company and deliver the product or service that your client has purchased from you. The personal guarantee is your warranty to the factoring client that you will be there if called upon to correct any problem with the product or service on the invoice you sold the factoring company so the factoring company will get paid on the factored invoice. If the factoring company does non-recourse factoring, you will not be asked to sign a personal guarantee.

Many of you will not want to sign the personal guarantee and go with a non-recourse factoring company and I will tell you that you are making a mistake unless you do not wish to warranty your product or service. Recourse only comes into play when you do not honor your obligations. Non-recourse factoring companies have more rules and stricter limits.

1. Security Ranking. Your business must be able to provide the factoring company with a first-place security charge on your receivables. The factoring company cannot buy receivables that you do not own and if you have pledged your invoices to another lender, you will not be able to sell them to the factoring company because you no longer own them.

2. Subordinating Securities. In situations where you have already pledged your receivables to another lender, you might be able to get that lender to subordinate their security into a second-place position, which would allow the factoring company to have a first-place charge on your receivables. This would allow them to factor your business. If the current lender is not willing to subordinate their security on your receivables, sometimes you will have enough outstanding receivables for the factoring company to buy and payout the other lender, which would allow the factoring company to move into a first-place security position on your receivables.

3. Sufficient Margins: You must have sufficient margin in your product or service to be able to handle the factoring fee. Each industry is different, and the size of your average invoice will play a part in determining if the factoring company feels your business can absorb the factoring fee. Generally, the factoring company will want you to have at least a 25% profit margin.

4. Creditworthy Clients: Will the creditworthy payer allow the payments to go to the factoring company or to a lock box bank account? A lock box at a bank is a bank account in your business's name that is controlled by the factoring company. The factoring company purchased the invoice and therefore owns the invoice, so they must be able to collect that payment directly. All large credit-worthy companies and governments pay factoring companies every day. If your client says they won't, stop selling to the client as this is a definite sign your client is in financial trouble.

* * * * *

Fast Forward Your Business Growth with Factoring

David was a potential new client of mine with a small business producing garbage bins for the commercial garbage bin business. He was approached by a large and reputable garbage bin company to produce bins for them. If David were to take this on, his business would immediately grow by 500%. Great news—however, the bad news was that David had no ability to finance the 500% increase in business. Without new financing David could not fill the new orders. David's accountant suggested he consider using factoring to finance it.

He started to investigate the business of factoring. Everything pointed to factoring being the financing solution he was looking for. David contacted my company, and we had a long discussion about how factoring worked. We explored whether it would work for his business…and the answer was, yes! Factoring would be perfect for financing the growth of his business. David was concerned his new client might worry about the financial strength of his business if he were to use factoring.

To alleviate his concerns (and those of many other new clients) I suggested he call his new potential client's head of accounts payable and ask, without giving his company name, if they had any rules about their clients using a factoring company.

Note: Never discuss factoring with the buyer. Call the accounts payable department to discuss this, unless they specifically ask, "Do you have the financing to produce the orders from our company?" If they do ask you, let them know you have financing from ABC Company (whatever the name of your factoring company is).

David contacted the head of accounts payable (AP) and asked if they had any rules or concerns about their clients using the services of a factoring company. The head of AP said, "we have no concerns and only one rule, which is that we need a letter of direction from you directing us to pay your factoring company."

Happy and relieved, David asked another question: "Why do you not care that my company uses a factoring company?" The answer was simple and straightforward. "David, we have chosen your company to produce the bins we need because you can deliver an excellent product in seven days and our current supplier takes 90 days. If you use a factoring company, we know you will have all the financing you need to produce our orders in the expected seven days. The faster you deliver, the faster we can put these bins out and make money from them. If sending the money to the factoring company (with the same payment terms) will enable you to deliver in seven days, why wouldn't we accommodate this? It's a win/ win situation."

The factoring arrangement was set up the next day, David's business grew quickly and profitably, and word got around about the quality of his bins and the speedy delivery, and David started to pick up new clients. Since factoring provided all the financing he needed, he was able to direct all his time to producing and delivering his bins instead of worrying about where he'd get the money to be able to say yes to new business, a problem so many small growing businesses have.

Another interesting thing happened that showed how lucrative a factoring relationship can be when a problem arises between the client and the payer. The waste management company had a policy on how they paid invoices. The invoice would be sent with the bin to the city it was delivered to. David was delivering to four different cities. The manager in each city signed off on the invoice and sent it to head office, which was situated in a fifth city, for payment. My factoring company was receiving payments on the account from three of the four cities between 15 and 30 days, but the fourth city was going over 90 days and still no payment would be received. I informed David that we would not factor the fourth city until receiving payment on all the outstanding invoices. I suggested he contact the head of AP and let him know he would no longer be delivering to that city. It's important to know that the factoring company has the right to call the AP department, but I have always given my clients the option of calling themselves.

David called the head of the AP department to let him know that the factoring company was not willing to purchase anymore invoices from that one location until all the invoices had been paid in full. The head of the AP was very upset to hear that the manager in that city was not doing his job. After looking into the matter, he got back to David and let him know that the problem was resolved and that there'd be no further delays; he should expect payment in two days for all outstanding invoices. Two days later, we were paid in full and there was never a problem again with payment from sales to that city.

By the way, the company grew so quickly and was so profitable because of factoring, that a competitor purchased David's business.

WHY IS FACTORING THE MOST POWERFUL FORM OF FINANCING BESIDES AN UNLIMITED LINE OF CREDIT FROM A BANK?

1. It alleviates collection problems. A factoring company will do its own credit checks on your clients and help you determine which of your clients are creditworthy and which ones you should either sell to on a COD basis, or not sell to at all. This will prevent your business from selling to a company you will have problems collecting from and thus make you more profitable. Many times, you will make more money saying NO to a potential client than saying YES to one who is either slow to pay, or who doesn't pay at all.

2. Factoring grows with you as fast your business grows. Technically you are selling COD while still giving 30-90 days credit to your clients.

3. A factoring company wants to buy every credit-worthy invoice you have. That is how they grow their own businesses. The more you're able to sell, the larger your business becomes.

4. Better cash flow. You never have to worry about tying-up your limited cash resources in large 30-90-day term invoices with large corporations.

- With consistent cash flow you can budget your business with more certainty

- With consistent cash flow you can take advantage of discounts that your suppliers offer for quick payment, or volume discounts for larger inventory purchasers

- With consistent cash flow you will reduce the enormous amount of time many business owners spend worrying about how they are going to pay their bills (payroll, rent, suppliers, long term obligations, etc.) and instead spend that time running and growing your business

5. Potential to secure more business. Factoring will help you secure more business from large corporations. Large corporations want to make sure you have the funds to produce or service the job they are looking to give you. They cannot afford to offer your business the contract and find out down the road that you do not have the funds to deliver the contract. Factoring tells them you have the resources to deliver.

6. Factoring will help you to secure bank financing down the road. You will be able to go into a bank and instead of what most businesses ask for—a line of credit to finance their business—you will be able to walk in and ask for less expensive financing

because you already have all the financing your business needs from the factoring company. If the bank will not provide everything you need, you can continue with the factoring company until the bank recognizes their mistake and sets up the line of credit. Banks love to take business away from other lenders. If other lenders are financing your business, your business must be working, so they are quick to move forward with your financing request.

THE MOST FREQUENT QUESTIONS PEOPLE ASK ABOUT FACTORING ARE:

1. How much does it cost?
2. Why do I have to sign a personal guarantee?
3. How fast does the factoring company advance funds?
4. Why does the factoring company have to collect the receivables when I can collect them and pass along the funds when my company is paid?
5. What are my clients going to think of my business if I'm using a factoring company?

HERE ARE SOME IMPORTANT DETAILS THAT WILL HELP ANSWER THOSE QUESTIONS:

1. Factoring companies usually ask for a one-year commitment. But every company is different. If the company doesn't set limits on the amount you have

to factor each month, then the one-year contract really becomes a one-year term during which you cannot switch to another factoring company. You don't want to be tied into a minimum usage contract, but if you can't avoid it, you'll want this agreement divided into three-month time periods.

2. The factoring company might require a minimum usage contract if your business represents a very small account. In this case the factoring company needs to justify the time spent on your account. Just as much work goes into buying a $1,000 invoice as a million-dollar invoice.

3. Very large companies might have to sign a minimum usage agreement because the factoring company will have to allocate funds to the account, and they don't want to pay interest on money that's sitting around doing nothing. A very large company would be one that probably has a factoring limit of more than $3,000,000. I would never sign a minimum usage agreement for a business looking for a $500K- $1,500,000 factoring limit. Find another factoring company if they insist on it.

4. Account setup. You might be asked to pay a one-time due diligence and legal fee for the setup of your account. If this is reasonable, there is nothing wrong with paying this fee. Generally, in 95% of the setups that fee should be between $500-$2,500. If your business is complicated, has a large volume of transactions, or is a public company, etc., the

factoring company might be justified in charging a larger setup fee. You might be able to negotiate a refund on the excess fees based on the volume of business you pass through the factoring company in your first year.

5. The best factoring companies to use are generally Canadian factoring companies. They tend to not have all the extra charges I mentioned earlier. They all have US accounts, so there are no worries regarding currency exchanges. The Canadian banking system runs much smoother than the American system, and the Canadian banks factoring companies use have thousands of branches throughout the United States. Canadian factoring companies will buy US receivables, but most US factoring companies will not buy Canadian receivables, unless they have an office in Canada.

6. Factoring advances. Most factoring companies will advance 80-85% of the gross amount of the invoice including any sales tax included in the invoice. Each industry is different, and it will also matter if you are using a recourse or non-recourse factoring company. In the temporary employment industry, for example, 90%+ is the norm and the advance might be less than 80-85% when you sell to big box stores.

7. The amount that is not advanced is called the "holdback" or the "reserve fund." The holdback/reserve fund is used to collect the fees the factoring company will be charging your business

on the invoice when it is paid. They will also use the holdback to cover any short payments your client makes on the invoice, as well as to create a reserve if one of your invoices is not paid. If an invoice is not paid or has a shortfall greater than the amount in the reserve for that invoice, the factoring company will take money out of the holdback/reserve funds of other invoices. The holdback/reserve will be returned to you—less factoring fees and short-falls—either the next day or whenever you have arranged with the factoring company for its return. Some factoring companies pay the holdback/ reserve the next day, a scheduled day each week or the next time you factor. This is your money and should always be available to you quickly.

8. Fees for factoring. Do factoring companies charge their fees on the gross invoice (100% of the invoice) or on the funds advanced? Generally, they charge on the gross invoice, not on the advanced amount. This is costlier but not a dealbreaker. What you need to do is compare all the fees being charged on your account, not just the factoring rate. Therefore, it's important to understand if there are fees on top of the factoring rate. Hidden fees are the killer when factoring, not the fee charged on the gross invoice.

9. What are today's fees? Generally, factoring companies range from 1.5% to 3%, and most are in the range of 1.75% to 2.25%. Are there lower fees? Yes, but your volume must be enormous—both in average invoice dollar amount and monthly volume. Very few businesses qualify for this and

most that would meet these requirements have bank financing.

10. Are the rates negotiable? Generally, not at the beginning of a relationship but at the beginning of the relationship you can negotiate a lower rate based on the business you give the factoring company over a specific period. This negotiated rate should kick in automatically when you have reached the milestones negotiated when you first signed up with the factoring company. They should be set out in writing, and you should not have to ask for them to be implemented, they should just happen automatically. Ask your broker to help negotiate these rate changes.

11. Don't get stuck. Never lock yourself into a deal you cannot get out of at the end of the contract (generally a one-year contract). Make sure there are no penalties for leaving at the end of the contract and that the factoring company can't automatically renew your contract for another year. If everything is going well, you and the factoring company don't need to renew the contract for you to continue factoring with them. They want you to stay so there is no need to sign a new contract unless the terms have drastically changed. Let your broker and your lawyer help with the decision to sign, or not to sign, a new one-year contract.

12. The factoring costs should be treated as an extra "salesperson" commission. Without the extra sales-person you wouldn't have the extra business. If you

don't have the extra business, you are not paying commission for the extra salesperson.

Now let's answer the last two most frequently asked questions about factoring.

WHY CAN'T A BUSINESS COLLECT FUNDS AND FORWARD THE MONEY TO THEIR FACTORING COMPANY?

A factoring company cannot allow a client to collect funds and forward them to the factoring company because the factoring company owns those receivables. They use those receivables as security with their lenders (factoring companies have lenders like other businesses do), and therefore they must have control of them. Unfortunately, history has shown that a client does not always immediately pass along the funds that they have mistakenly collected to the factoring company. The number one excuse that a factoring company hears is *"my secretary or the junior person in our accounting department didn't know and deposited it."* That does happen sometimes, but most of the time the client deposits funds because they're desperate for cash flow and figure they'll provide the factoring company another invoice later to cover the one they collected but didn't return immediately to the factoring company. They figure they're paying interest, so it doesn't matter. But it does matter and cannot be allowed.

AND, FINALLY, WHAT WILL YOUR CLIENTS THINK IF YOU ARE USING A FACTORING COMPANY?

The biggest concern potential new factoring clients have before they sign up is around what their clients will think of their business if they're factoring. They ask, "Won't they think I'm in financial trouble and that is why I use a factoring company?"

This is a great question, but the answer is *no*. They will think the opposite is true. Without this financing your business won't grow. In fact, it might even fail because your business gains a reputation as one that cannot deliver. Remember, the number one reason that you use a factoring company is because your business is growing or has the potential to grow faster than its present financing can handle.

This is not to say that every employee who works for your new client understands what factoring is and that is why you only discuss factoring with the head of accounts payable.

A Factoring Success Story

Tony was in a specialized trucking business with about six very large companies for whom his company supplied direct shipping services. Tony was running the business and he had a silent partner who wanted to be bought out.

There was a $125,000 line of credit on the business that was secured by a collateral mortgage on Tony's in-laws' house. Tony's in-laws had only agreed to securing the line of credit for one year, but the security had now been in place for more than two years, and this was causing Tony a family problem. Meanwhile, Tony had neither the money to buy out his silent partner nor the ability to replace the collateral mortgage used as security for the line of credit. The bank also had a first-place security (GSA) on the business even though they had the collateral mortgage. Banks will generally take the extra security even when the loan is fully secured.

Even though the silent partner's offer of $120,000 for the business was a fair one ($60,000 down and $5,000 monthly for 12 months), Tony didn't have the money to buy the partner's shares and he couldn't go to the bank as they were not prepared to extend any credit to the company without hard security.

Tony first approached my company to lend him the money to buy the shares, but I was in the factoring business not the loan business, so that was not a financing I could accommodate. The receivables were exactly what my factoring company loved to factor, however. They were very high quality and a decent, average, size. However, the bank owned the security, so it was not possible for my company to factor them. Then I came up with an idea I hoped would work for all parties. If my company were able to factor Tony's company's existing receivables, that would provide the down payment for the shares and then Tony could factor the new invoices for his working capital.

The first hurdle was to deal with the bank that held a security charge on the company's assets, which included the receivables. I had to get the bank to subordinate their security charge on the receivables. Since the bank had hard security on the business through the collateral mortgage, they were willing to subordinate on the receivables. This would allow my company to register a first-place charge on the receivables and allow us to factor Tony's company. First problem solved.

The next discussion was with the silent partner. The silent partner owned 50% of the shares in the business and Tony owned the other 50%. Tony and I needed the partner to allow Tony to control all the shares of the business so he could register his business for factoring.

So, you might be wondering, "Why would the silent partner give Tony his shares without getting fully paid for them?" Well, the partner wanted out and the only way was to either find a buyer to take the entire business or take a reasonable risk on our plan to pay him in full over one year. Since this was a friendly sale between two friends, he took a risk on the purchase arrangement I put forward.

We offered to put 100% of the shares in trust with the silent partner's lawyer and also give a third-place GSA on the company. This was actually a second-place *charge as the bank was secured through a collateral mortgage. Tony, through factoring, would be able to make the down payment to purchase the silent partner's shares, which represented 50% of the sale price. He'd have the cashflow needed to run the business and make his monthly payments through factoring the company's new invoices. The silent partner would hold 100% of the shares on a one-year payout loan that represented only 25% of the then-current value of the company ($240,000). Each month $5,000 of the remaining purchase amount would be paid to the silent partner.*

If Tony was unable to make all payments for the remaining 50% of the purchase price, the silent partner had the right to sell the entire business in order to re-coup the remaining amount owned on the share purchase. Second problem solved.

Everything worked out perfectly. At the end of one year the company had grown to the point that the silent partner was completely paid off, the bank released the collateral mortgage that was being used to secure the operating line of credit and they doubled the line of credit for the business. The only bad thing was for me: Tony's business no longer needed factoring.

This is a great example of how factoring isn't used only to finance the growth of the business, but it can also help purchase shares in the business—and to do so with no money out of the owner's pocket.

* * * * *

Another Factoring Success Story

Meet Joe. Joe owned a computer chip business. He purchased computer chips from the United States and brought them to Canada to sell to computer manufacturers. Among other things, factoring companies look for enough margin in a business's product or service to absorb the factoring costs and, generally, that minimum should be at least 25%. Joe presented me with a factoring situation that went against that scenario and when he approached my company for factoring, I had to turn him down. His margin was only between 10-12%. Even though this was higher than most companies selling computer chips, it was not enough for factoring.

Joe asked me to reconsider. He wanted me to do the due diligence on the two companies he wanted to factor. Since the invoices were going to be between $50,000 and $250,000—with sales of $500,000 to $1,000,000 a month, I agreed to investigate it. And was I glad I did. The due diligence showed two very creditworthy computer manufactures and excellent average-sized invoices. However, there still wasn't enough margin.

I explained to Joe that my company would love to factor his receivables, but his margins were too small. I could only advance 80% of the receivables, which would mean he'd have to put money into every deal. I also said that on a receivable with a 10% margin that went 30 days, I'd be making 30% of the profit and if it went 60 days, then I'd make 60% of the profit (rates were much higher then). This didn't make sense to me, since factoring companies generally make 5-15% of the margin, not 30-60%.

Joe really wanted this. He came back with two points to persuade me to agree. One: he had no problem putting in the shortfall on each deal if my company would only advance 80% on each invoice. That was great but not a deal maker. And two, (which sealed the deal): he said that on a million dollars in receivables—where my company would earn 30% of his profit—he'd earn 70%, which would work out to $70,000 a month. He'd rather have my company factor his million dollars a month to earn $70,000 than not have that business at all. He was happy to pay my company $30,000 if by doing so he earned $70,000.

I said yes, and in that first year he sold over $16,000,000 in computer chips and made more than $1,000,000.

Sometimes in business you need to think outside the box. There is no bigger financing business that thinks outside the box than a factoring company. Bring them a creditworthy payer whose payments they can control, and they will take you on. If they don't, call me and I will.

FACTORING VERSUS BANK FINANCING

Which is more costly, factoring or bank financing? And how do you determine that? Is it by seeing how much the lender charges, or by how much a business can earn by using one lender over another? I say it's by how much money you make, how big your business gets, and the reputation you build with your clients.

Here's a scenario I like to use when presenting how a factoring company charging 3% a month (36% a year) is much cheaper than a bank charging 3% a year. So that we compare apples to apples we'll look at **Hypothetical Company A and Hypothetical Company B.** Every sale of each company is $100,000, with a $30,000 profit margin.

The costs of manufacturing come to $70,000 for each order and payment terms are 60 days from delivery. Each company has $100,000 in working capital.

Company A also has a $100,000 line of credit from the bank that is marginable at 65%. This means they can only borrow 65% of every invoice until they reach their $100,000 line of credit limit.

Company B has a factoring relationship on top of their $100,000 in cash to finance their receivables at 80% (the standard factoring advance rate) of the gross amount of the invoice.

On sale one, each company draws from their $100,000 cash to fulfill their first order, leaving each with $30,000 to put towards general expenses such as rent and other office expenses.

On sale two, **Company A** draws down $65,000 from their operating line of credit (the max they can margin their bank line of credit) and uses $5,000 from their remaining $30,000 company cash. They margined the first $100,000 in order to produce the second order.

Company B factors the first invoice and receives $80,000 from the factoring company to produce the second order.

The third order comes in and **Company A** only has $35,000 left to draw down on their line of credit and $25,000 from the internal funds, less all general expenses from month one and what will be needed for month two.

Company A	Invoice Amount	Gross Profit	Financing Cost	Net Profit
Sale #1	$100,000	$30,000	0	$30,000
Sale #2	$100,000	$30,000	$325	$29,675
Sale #3	0	0	0	0
Sale #4	0	0	0	0
Sale #5	0	0	0	0
Sale #6	0	0	0	0
Sale #7	0	0	0	0
Sale #8	0	0	0	0
Sale #9	0	0	0	0
60-day totals	$200,000	$60,000	$325	$59,675

Therefore, **Company A** does not have enough money to produce order number three unless the bank will increase their line of credit. The bank is not going to increase the line of credit on a new business and tells the company that when they receive payment from their first order, they will have enough money to produce the third order. There's only one problem with that: the customer will not wait the 60 days for **Company A** to get paid in order to deliver the third purchase order. Result? Lost business and most likely a lost client.

Company B factors the second invoice and receives $80,000 and uses it to deliver the third order. **Company B** continues factoring each order and delivers new orders

Company B	Invoice Amount	Gross Profit	Financing Cost	Net Profit
Sale #1	$100,000	$30,000	$6,000	$24,000
Sale #2	$100,000	$30,000	$6,000	$24,000
Sale #3	$100,000	$30,000	$6,000	$24,000
Sale #4	$100,000	$30,000	$6,000	$24,000
Sale #5	$100,000	$30,000	$6,000	$24,000
Sale #6	$100,000	$30,000	$6,000	$24,000
Sale #7	$100,000	$30,000	$6,000	$24,000
Sale #8	$100,000	$30,000	$6,000	$24,000
Sale #9	$100,000	$30,000	$0.00	$30,000
60-day totals	$900,000	$270,000	$48,000	$222,000

every week for nine weeks. On the ninth week they do not need factoring and do not factor the ninth order.

Company A has only paid the bank $325 in interest for the 60 days the bank's money was out and made a profit of $59,675 on the two orders they were able to deliver. They do not have any more orders because their clients cannot count on them to deliver.

Company B has paid the factoring company $48,000 to factor eight of their nine invoices but has made a profit on the nine invoices of $222,000 and continues to receive orders from their clients.

The factoring company charged $48,000, versus the bank, which charged $325. But who was really more expensive—the factoring company that charged $48,000 but allowed **Company B** to earn $222,000 in 60 days, or the bank that charged $325 but earned **Company A** only $59,675 and cost them clients because they could not deliver quickly?

Are you in business to make money, or to see how little interest you can pay? You are in business to make money, so stop worrying about how much interest you pay for your financing. Worry about how much money you are making and how many clients you have.

CHAPTER 6

Purchase Order Financing and Letters of Credit

Much as factoring can solve an awful lot of a business's cash flow and growth problems, there are still two more options that I feel it's important to talk about: purchase order financing and letters of credit. Get a handle on how these work so you can make even better decisions for your business going forward and avoid a lot of the problems that plague a lot of businesses that ultimately end up closing their doors. For good. In this chapter we're going to look at Purchase Order Financing.

PURCHASE ORDER FINANCING

Purchase Order Financing (POF) is when a third party lends money or credit to help you get the product(s) you need to fulfill orders when you are not able to get credit for yourself.

You work hard to get a new client to give you an order. They finally deliver your dream purchase order. Now it's time to produce the order. You contact your supplier for the materials you need. The supplier says your order is over your credit limit with them, and you'll have to pay 50% up front and the other 50% when said order is ready to be delivered. Great. You don't have the 50% down payment now, and you won't have the 50% when the order is ready. What to do? Unless your supplier delivers the materials you need your business will lose not only the order, but a new client as well.

You promise you'll pay them when you get paid. They say no to the credit increase. You can't understand why not because if they do, they'll do more business. Aren't they in business to do business? Without the extended credit they lose out on the sale and the profit. That may be true, but in their minds, they see extending you more credit as a credit risk. Why is that? How can they know that you will:

> a) deliver the order to the client that you said the order is for, and not to a different client? and
>
> b) pay them when you get paid?

Even with your best intentions and all the integrity in the world, here are some reasons you might not pay them when you get paid:

Situation 1: You have other obligations that you pay before, or instead of the supplier.

Situation 2: You get another order and found a less expensive supplier, but that supplier wants to be paid COD.

Situation 3: You decide that your business is not a good one and you keep the money and close the business.

In the first two situations, you figure you'll just pay the supplier from the proceeds of your next sale. You might even think to yourself that you're prepared to pay some interest for taking longer than you first promised. And, in the third situation, you decide to protect your best interests and move onto something else, leaving behind unfulfilled orders and unpaid bills.

Suppliers do not stay in business by offering credit to businesses that do not deserve credit. New businesses do not deserve large credit limits. So, how do you get large credit limits if your business does not qualify? You go to a company that provides purchase order (PO) financing.

PURCHASE ORDER FINANCING IS PROVIDED BY

1. A PO company that will most likely want a factoring company to pay them out from the invoice that will be created by their PO financing or

2. A factoring company that provides PO financing. It is generally more expensive than factoring, especially if it is provided by a purchase order financing company, rather than a factoring company that does purchase order financing.

Here's an example of a situation where purchase order financing can save the day:

A large grocery chain wants a new jam company's product and issues a $300,000 purchase order for delivery in six weeks. The new company does not have a facility that can produce a $300,000 order, let alone in six weeks, and even if it had the facility, it does not have the money to buy the supplies to produce the order. So, what can the owners do? How do they get this order produced if they can't produce it themselves? They find a third-party manufacturer to produce the order with their recipe. Companies like the large grocery chain that placed this $300,000 jam order buy products made by third-party food manufacturers every day without even knowing it.

So, this new jam company finds a company that can manufacture the order to their specification (their recipe) within the allotted time. They are very excited. They do not have to be bothered with buying the ingredients, the jars, the labels, or even delivering the product…and they are going to make more than $100,000 on an order someone else is going to manufacture and deliver for them. Then the party is over before it really started. The manufacturer says they need $50% up front and 50% COD. What can this company do now? The order is due in six weeks, and they've used all their money just to get to this point.

Let's see what this jam business has:

1. A large order.
2. Good profit margins.
3. A manufacturer able to deliver on time.
4. A creditworthy payer.
5. A factoring company willing to buy the invoice.

The factoring company wants to buy the invoice, but they can't because the order can't be produced without paying 50% up front and having 50% available before delivery. Factoring companies buy receivables; they do not lend money. The manufacturer wants to produce the order but is not about to give $200,000 in credit to a brand-new company.

This is where a purchase order financing company comes to the rescue.

The PO company approaches the manufacturer and tries to arrange credit for the order. They offer to pay the manufacturer the day after the grocery chain receives and accepts the order. Along with getting a $200,000 order that they had previously turned down because of credit issues, the manufacturer will also get paid one day after the order is accepted by the grocery chain—which is 30-60 days sooner than they get paid by the clients to whom they have extended credit.

However, they still must extend credit to the PO company, so they do credit work on the PO company and almost every time they extend the credit. What happens if they won't extend the credit to the PO company? Then the PO finance company arranges payment to the manufacturer either through a letter of credit or by putting the money into a trust account with a large law firm approved by the manufacturer. However, the conditions do not change: the manufacturer will get paid one day after the grocery chain accepts the order, but only if they accept the order. If for any reason, the grocery chain does not accept the order, the PO company does not sign off and the funds are not released.

Something else is important in this potential transaction and that is confirmation that this manufacturer is the right one for the job. Only a manufacturer that can deliver will take on this order, since they can only get paid if the order is delivered and accepted by the grocery chain. If everything goes to plan and the order is delivered and accepted by the grocery chain, the PO finance company signs off and the manufacturer gets paid. The PO company is paid quickly by the factoring company that buys the invoice. The factoring company sends the PO company their funds and fees, gives the client the difference between what the PO company is due from the 80% factoring advance, and waits to get paid by the grocery chain.

The client now has a business, a manufacturer to produce their orders so they don't have to set up their own manufacturing plant, and all the financing they need to meet all the orders that come their way.

This is what is called a win for everyone: The client gets to deliver an order without having any money, the manufacturer gets a new client without credit risk and a bonus of quick payment, the PO company gets a new client, the factoring company gets a new client, and the grocery chain gains a new product for their customers.

A Purchase Order Financing Success Story

David worked for a print broker as a salesperson for several years and now he wants to go out on his own. He has the experience and the contacts, but he doesn't realize he needs money to get orders produced. He never had to worry about financing when he was working for someone else as his company had credit with all their suppliers, so it never occurred to him that he would not be extended at least some credit.

David starts his business on Monday, telling everyone he knows that he is now on his own and ready to help with all their printing needs.

The next day, he gets a call from a friend who works for a well-known gas company. A $500,000 job is being offered for tender and it's a big one. David bids and wins the job. He knows exactly who he wants to do the printing for the job, and he approaches them. They give him a great price of $300,000 to deliver the job and he's already counting his $200,000 in profit.

Then he gets the call from the printing company's credit department to inform him that they need 50% up front and 50% on delivery. "But you know me! We've been doing business for years without any problems so why do you need the money up front?" The credit department answers, "We have been doing business with your former employer, not with you and your new business."

What's David going to do now, with nothing more than bus fare in his pocket? He approaches his family and friends but although they believe in him, they do not have that kind of money to lend him. He approaches the bank, but he has no security to offer for a loan. They say they can't lend him any money but would be happy to set up a new business account for him.

He calls his business broker—one of his new business's team members—for help and this is one good reason why a broker is part of new business's team. The broker suggests that everything can be solved quite easily through purchase order financing and factoring.

Just as with the jam business scenario, the purchase order company arranges the credit with the printer and the job is produced, delivered, and accepted by the gas company. The factoring company buys the invoices, pays the PO company back the $300,000 they paid the printer plus fees, and gives the remaining money from the $400,000 available from the factoring company to David. When the factoring company gets paid, they return the 20% held back from the invoice less their fees. David, with no money, earns $200,000 less the fees on his first job. Not bad for a brand-new business with no money or credit, right?

If 60-90 days passed between the time the PO company put the money out until the time the factoring company received payment on the invoice, the cost to David would have been $20,000 to $40,000. Expensive, true. But when you can make $160,000-$180,000 without *you or your business having any money or credit, is it really?* **The PO and factoring company fees are just a sales commission on a job that would never have been completed without their involvement.**

Never worry about how much someone else is making, only worry about how much you are making. You can also think of this as having a partner on the deal but not in your business, or that you are just charging less to your client.

Here is another situation where I helped a client with PO financing. The client was in the zinc die casting business making electrical connectors. When I first started to factor the account, the company was on a COD basis with the zinc supplier because they owed them $120,000 that they could not pay. The company really started to grow. Within six months of starting to factor their receivables they went from $100,000 per month in sales to $300,000 a month, and within two years they were selling $500,000-$600,000 a month. With the growth came the need for much larger volumes of zinc per month. Eventually this client would be purchasing 180,000 pounds of zinc monthly.

Since the receivables were going up and the reserve (holdback) on the receivables was generally in the $150,000-plus range, I was confident enough to arrange with the zinc supplier that I would not only guarantee the zinc deliveries but would guarantee a zinc contract for 2,500,000 pounds of zinc at 62.5 cents a pound (the zinc market had crashed).

My company and the zinc company had to agree on some conditions. From my side, the conditions were:

1. No zinc could be delivered without my signing off on the order and

2. That we could replace shipments with spot purchases—i.e., when the price of zinc was low, we could buy it at the spot price instead of using up some of our 62.5-cent contract price.

The zinc company wanted the remaining outstanding debt to be immediately paid in full (there was only about $40,000 left at the time). And they wanted all the payments to come from my company, not the zinc company. These were easy conditions for both sides to live with and we struck a deal.

How did I protect myself entering into the agreement with the zinc company, given that my factoring company was on the hook for any zinc that was purchased? Here's how:

1. I had a first-place security agreement on my client's entire company.

2. I controlled the zinc shipments.

3. The holdback account always had more than enough holdback in it for what was owing to the zinc supplier.

4. I controlled all the receivables.

5. If the company collapsed, I could have a problem with the rest of the zinc contract, but my only concern would have been the difference between my contract of 62.5 cents and if zinc were selling

for less than that. Turns out that zinc only went up after we signed our contract. So, within months we were saving thousands in zinc costs because of the contract and that turned into $20,000 a month before the contract was even six months old.

The client used factoring to grow their business and third-party guarantees (an interesting form of purchase order financing) to save money on the Number One product they needed in their business. The savings on the zinc contract were greater than the factoring fees they were paying during the contract.

This was a great win for everyone. The client grew and made more money because of increased sales and lower costs, the zinc company now had a good client buying more and paying on time, and my factoring company did more business.

WHILE WE'RE TALKING ABOUT POFS, LET'S TAKE A SHORT DETOUR INTO THE WORLD OF LETTERS OF CREDIT

When you issue a letter of credit through a bank, you give the money directly to the bank and they put it into their letter-of-credit account. They need to have the money because they are issuing the letter of credit on your behalf but since the money is coming directly from them they want your money in their bank account—not yours—so it will still be there when needed.

Although straightforward, letters of credit can become dangerous when not done properly. The first letter of credit I was involved with was for me. I was buying goods from the Philippines and the supplier wanted a letter of credit in place before they would produce the order. I met with a bank manager to help arrange the letter of credit. Lucky for me he didn't know what he was doing. He explained that I had to set up a bank account and put the money into it, and it would be drawn on when the letter of credit was cashed. This is not correct, not that I knew it at the time.

The letter of credit was drawn up, the beneficiary being the supplier in the Philippines. The letter detailed what the supplier was shipping to me (colors, sizes, quantities, etc.) and the date by which the goods had to be shipped. The bank manager wanted me to agree to an open letter of credit. This meant that the supplier could send the goods whenever he wanted to. This made no sense to me, so I didn't agree to it. We put a fixed date on the letter of credit and if the goods were not shipped by that day, I could either cancel the order or extend the shipping date.

Good thing I didn't listen to the bank manager. The goods did not leave by the due date and the supplier had to reach out to me to extend the shipping date. He said he need two days, so I extended it two days. The order was small, so I was shipping it by air. The shipment was to take two days to get to me. Back then you could not follow your shipment by the hour like you can today. Apparently, the shipment left on the second day, but the supplier did not get to his bank until the day after the due date. The next day—now four days beyond the expected shipping date—I received a call from the bank manager asking me to extend the due date again. I asked what would happen if I did not sign the extension. Would the money sit in limbo forever? He said in principle it would stay there until I signed the necessary extension or release. I told the bank manager I'd let him know what I planned to do after I spoke with the supplier.

I needed to find the goods, but the airline could not help me. The goods were on the way, but no one knew exactly where they were. Remember, the bank manager had me set up a bank account to hold the funds for the letter of credit, but the bank never took the money out. Since I couldn't track the goods and the letter of credit was in limbo, I took the bulk of the money and put it in my personal account at another bank. The goods finally arrived three days after the due date. When I opened the boxes up to my surprise only about 50% of the goods matched what I had ordered. The rest were replacement items.

The situation was now all in my favor. The supplier in the Philippines had a stale-dated letter of credit worth nothing. I had the goods, the money, and three choices:

1. Let the letter of credit go through even though I did not get everything I ordered.

2. Pay nothing and keep the goods and the money. Or

3. Pay for only the items that arrived as ordered.

I went with Option #3: pay for what was delivered correctly. I contacted the supplier by telex (if you're asking what a telex is, you're very young and it doesn't matter), and told him there would be no more telexes, he could call me directly. He called that night. I told him, "You sent 50% of the order correctly and the rest was substituted." He asked me to ship everything back and I told him to send me my $900 for shipping charges and whatever I had to pay to get the goods to him." He said he would pay me after he received the goods. I explained, "Well, I live 12,000 miles away and I have both the goods and the money. You can accept 50% payment representing the goods that came in correctly or get nothing." There was a little delay while he thought about it and guess what? He accepted the deal.

What I learned on my first experience with letter of credits: be aware of what you put in your documentation. If you can get the goods inspected, do so. In fact, on large orders, you must. Never have an open shipping date on the letter of credit. Finally, before you issue a letter of credit, ask the bank what the minimum charge is for the LOC and don't pay more than that amount. Banks will try to charge a percentage of the value of the letter of credit which makes no sense whatsoever. It does not cost more money to put extra "0's" in the letter of credit.

CHAPTER 7

Leasing

I bet you're starting to figure out that there are a lot of options available for financing your business and that having an out-of-the-box thinker on your team who knows about these opportunities could really help you a) stay afloat and b) expand your business. This is part of why I love business. It's an endlessly creative project that includes some predictably logical processes. So, now let's look at leasing, the cash flow protector.

WHY LEASE YOUR EQUIPMENT AND HOW DOES LEASING WORK?

Many of you lease your vehicles. Why do you lease instead of buying?

1. When you lease, you don't have to lay out large dollar amounts, like you do if you choose to buy your vehicle.

2. You get more for your money when you are only paying part of the entire price of the vehicle off. Generally, at the end of the average vehicle lease of three-to-four years you have paid only 40-50% of the original cost of the vehicle. Yes, you paid

interest, but dealership interest is generally less than bank interest, so you are saving money and making smaller payments.

3. You get to give back the vehicle at the end of the lease without having to find a buyer, or you can choose to buy the vehicle at the end of the lease at a predetermined price.

4. You get a new vehicle every three-to-four years.

Leasing equipment for your business is pretty much the same as leasing a vehicle. You get the equipment you need with little or no outlay of principal. You might even buy a better and more expensive piece of equipment just because you are laying out first and last payments instead of having to pay 100% of the price of the equipment. Although equipment is the most popular use of a lease, you can also lease certain software.

WHERE DO YOU GET A LEASE?

Your team broker will have leasing contacts, and the place where you buy your equipment will generally send their clients to at least one leasing company. Sometimes banks will do leases for their current business clients, as well. Generally, a leasing company is looking to finance the entire cost of the piece of equipment, however, several issues will determine if they finance 100% of the total price:

1. Does your business qualify for the entire amount of the loan?

2. How specialized is the piece of equipment?

3. Did you buy the equipment or did the leasing company buy it?

Like every loan a business tries to acquire, the lender will decide how much, if any, of the loan they are prepared to advance, based on what a review of your business tells them. Like every loan a lender makes, they must take into consideration how they get their money back if the loan is not paid in full. Before deciding what percentage up to 100% of the cost of the equipment they are prepared to finance, the leasing company will take into consideration the resale value of the equipment, assuming they had to sell it back into the market to get their money back. When purchasing a piece of equipment that is very specialized, the leasing company most likely will not advance 100% of the cost of the equipment unless your credit is very good. If the piece of equipment is very common—like a car, truck, restaurant equipment etc.—then they are more likely to finance 100% of the cost of the item.

This is very important. A high percentage of leasing companies want to buy the item you want to lease directly and then lease it to you. Some will even consider your piece of equipment as used if you buy it and then want to lease it, even if it is still in the box unopened. If they treat it as used equipment, they will charge you a higher rate of interest. So, before you buy anything you are thinking of leasing, find a leasing company and ask about their rules.

Leasing is a great way to save your limited cash resources but be cautious before entering into any lease, just like you should be cautious entering into any agreement. The term of a lease will depend on the type of equipment you are buying. Generally, leases are for three years but they can run anywhere from one to 10 years. Some have large buybacks at the end of the lease, some have a very small buyback (as low as $1), some just continue charging you at the end of the lease a rental amount that is the same price you were paying—until you realize that the lease is over (you don't want to work with leasing companies that have that policy). Others do not include a buyback, you just own the equipment. Everything is negotiable, so have your team broker sit down with you and discuss what's best for your company, not the leasing company.

Leasing is one of the last popular forms of financing that has no rules or regulations. You need to read and understand what you are signing (bring in your team lawyer here) and how you want to set the lease up in order to take advantage of any tax savings (ask your team accountant).

WHAT ARE THE RATES FOR LEASING? AGAIN, IT DEPENDS ON VARIOUS FACTORS, SUCH AS:

1. How long have you been in business?
2. How is your businesses credit and how is your personal credit?
3. Are you dealing directly with the lender or through a leasing broker?
4. Is your equipment a common item or a specialty item?
5. What is the length of your lease?
6. How expensive is your piece of equipment?
7. Where are you getting the equipment, domestically or from overseas?
8. Have you ever leased from the lender before?

A brand-new company is not in a great negotiating position and should just be happy the leasing company is going to lease the equipment, within reason, of course. Generally, the interest rate is between 6-12%.

If your business has good credit, then at the current leasing rates you might be looking at 4%-9%. You also may be asked to give a personal guarantee, so use that to try and negotiate a lower rate. Make sure your team lawyer is involved before signing any documents. Make sure your team accountant looks at the actual costs of the lease because the interest rate is not always the entire fee. If there is a broker involved, their fee will be added to the overall cost of the piece of equipment. There is nothing wrong with the broker charging a fee, just be aware of it.

Dealing directly with the lender will sometimes lower the overall costs of financing but not necessarily. Not all lenders will deal directly with borrowers, however, when possible, try to deal with the lender directly.

If your piece of equipment is a speciality order, your interest rate is probably going to be a little higher and you might even have to make a down payment on it. You also have less opportunity to negotiate—unless you are a very large company and have some history with the leasing company—as there are fewer lenders that will lend on a special-order piece of equipment.

With a common piece of equipment, you (i.e., your team broker) will have an opportunity to negotiate, as there are many more lenders interested in your lease.

The length of your lease is something you need to discuss with you team accountant first to see how it fits into your budget. Generally speaking, the shorter the lease, the lower the interest rate but the higher the monthly payments. Your team accountant will help you determine if you are better off paying a lower interest rate over a shorter term with larger monthly payments, or a higher rate over a longer term with lower payments.

More expensive equipment may result in a slightly lower rate of interest. There is the same amount of work involved in the administration of every lease, however, the more expensive the equipment the fewer leases the company must administer to exhaust all their funds available for leases. Therefore, the administration cost per lease is a much smaller percentage of the overall costs on a lease and therefore the company is making more money. As well, generally, the bigger the lease the fewer problems that come with it since a company buying a large piece of equipment tends to be in good financial shape.

Getting a piece of equipment from overseas presents several problems that a domestic piece of equipment doesn't. Here's why:

1. It takes longer to get.
2. You must put the money up before you get the equipment.
3. If the item is not exactly as you ordered it could be challenging to rectify the situation.
4. Servicing might be an issue.

Even if the overseas equipment is ready for shipping, it needs to get to the boat, cross the ocean, and get through the port—and customs. Next, it must be delivered to your business, which could be across the country. Assuming everything goes smoothly at all checkpoints, you're looking at a minimum of a month before you can take delivery. However, that's a best-case scenario.

Oftentimes, the equipment is not available exactly on the day you order it and then when it's ready for shipping, the boat leaves a week or more later. I can tell you that no matter what port it arrives at, things don't run smoothly

100% of the time and it could be weeks before the equipment is eventually cleared by customs (and a customs broker will be needed at an additional cost to you). At last, after a harrowing journey, your equipment is on land again and then it must make its way to you. So, I'd say two-to-three months for delivery would be terrific, but you could be looking at up to six months, plus the added costs of shipping, insurance, and financing.

If you're lucky, the financing charges for the overseas purchase will start when the equipment is on the boat but 99% of the time, the financing starts when the order is placed. The manufacturer will want to be paid up front. This is something I highly recommend you don't do. You will be asked for a down payment, which I also recommend against. Instead of a down payment, put up a letter of credit for the entire amount. I recommend this for two reasons. First, I never want to give a down payment for something I can't control. What are you going to do if they take too long to ship—or worse, do not ship? The second reason is that this is a test. If a business will only do business with you if you send a down payment instead of a letter of credit for the full amount, that company has their own financing problems. You don't want to do business with an overseas company that does not have enough financing to produce your piece of equipment. The letter of credit solves the manufacturer's need to ensure they will get paid for their equipment.

Bear in mind, however, that the interest charges start once a letter of credit goes up. So, if the equipment takes three months to get to you from overseas, you have been charged an extra three months in interest.

And what are going to do if the equipment does not come in as expected? Easy answer: there is not much you can do. If you're lucky, there will be a domestic company that can possibly help correct the problem. If not, you have a very expensive unusable piece of equipment you are going to be paying for until the lease is finished.

You receive the equipment, and everything goes fine, until it doesn't. It's expensive to hire a repair company that does not represent the manufacturer to fix the equipment.

How do you resolve all these problems? Simple: buy domestically. This doesn't mean that the equipment is not made overseas, it just means that the manufacturer has representation domestically. When I say domestically, I mean in either the United States or Canada. If you want the equipment, you order it and it's delivered to you. The cost of financing is not relevant, since the longest it can take to get to your company is a week. The leasing company should have sufficient credit to have the equipment delivered to you before they pay for it, if not, one week of interest is a lot less than three months-plus.

If the company is represented domestically but you still need to order the equipment from overseas, a deposit might still be required. Leave that to the leasing company. They are smart enough and large enough to either get credit, put up the deposit domestically by way of a deposit to a lawyer's trust account, or through a letter of credit.

If you bought the equipment domestically and something is wrong with the equipment you can return it and if you can't return it the warranty will take care of everything. If it does not come with a warranty, then it's unlikely the lender will finance something you shouldn't be buying anyway.

If something breaks, the warranty will cover the company that is licensed to repair the equipment. If down the road the equipment is out of warranty, there will still be a licensed company available to do the repairs.

The leasing company is going to take security on the equipment for sure, but they might look for a personal guarantee from you and they might want to take security on your company. Security on the equipment does not matter to you or your company, so that is not something to even discuss. Taking your personal guarantee is something to take into consideration. If you're a small and/or new company, you may not have any choice but to sign it. Security on your company is another matter and should absolutely be discussed with your team lawyer. I would highly recommend not giving the corporate security to them other than on the piece of equipment, especially if they're looking to take security on your receivables.

Once they have security on your receivables, you've greatly limited your ability to borrow money from a bank, factoring company, or another lender. You might make an agreement to allow them to take a second-place charge on the receivables or at least have that written into the agreement to allow other lenders a first-place charge on your company's receivables. They might insist that the list they'll subordinate to is a short one, only including certain lenders such as a bank, a factoring company, or other cash lenders.

Leasing is a great form of financing, not just for a new business with limited cash but for any business. As with any lending you take on, have your team lawyer review all documents before signing.

What Can Happen When Borrowing Without Having a Lawyer and an Accountant Look at the Leases

This is the true story of the owners of a successful restaurant and two other food-related businesses who for the sake of this story we will call the Marco brothers. They decide to open another similar restaurant in what should have been a no-chance-to-fail location. When the leasing companies asked the owners to cross-collateralize all the leases against the other three businesses, they said "yes." The cross-collateralizing that the leasing companies wanted meant they had registered security on the other three businesses for all the leases on the new restaurant. This meant that if the new restaurant were unable to pay the new leases, then the leasing companies could and would go after the other three businesses for payment.

Well, guess what? The restaurant was in trouble from the day it opened. The lease payments were staggering, and the business never took off. Eventually the new business had to seek financial help from the other three businesses in order to meet their monthly obligations, in addition to the lease payments. As the months went by, the other three businesses started to feel the pinch of having to cover the expenses of the new restaurant.

At the end of the first year, the owners' accountant called me in to see if there was anything I could do to stop the financial bleeding. After reviewing the leases and other obligations, my conclusion was that all four businesses were now in jeopardy and immediate action was required.

The first thing we did was close the new restaurant. Then we checked to see if there was a way to address the equipment leases and the restaurant rental lease. I was able to get the owners out of the rental lease easily, but that was not the case with the equipment leases.

The owners had a total of eight equipment leases ranging from $25,000 to $300,000, adding up to $800,000 plus taxes. Approximately $200,000 had been paid off in the first year which left $600,000 plus taxes on the remaining leases. The $200,000 paid off in the first year represented the fees charged to *arrange the leases (they are added to the overall price of the equipment), the interest, and some principal.*

The client had properties that could be leveraged to secure about $450,000 in second mortgage funds (this is not usually available). I now calculated what the real principal was left on the leases and prepared a proposal for each of the leasing companies. Each company was offered the same percentage for the remaining balance of the lease they held. This was not a formal proposal through a Trustee, so no company could hold up the proposal by voting against it. I made it very clear that there was only so much money available so there would be no negotiating. Basically, you either accepted the offer and you were paid out or you could sue and see if you were successful in court years down the road.

The offer was extremely fair, it was for 65% of the remaining balance which represented about 90% of the principal owing. Since the principal was getting returned and the money could be re-invested in new deals, the interest loss was minor as it would be made up on the new deals that would earn the lender new fees for arranging a new lease.

Interestingly, the companies with the smallest and the largest leases took the deal immediately. Their only condition was that every lease get the same percentage payout. The two medium lease deals, ranging from $50,000-$100,000, didn't want to settle. One leasing company thought they could hold up the proposal until I explained that this was not a formal *proposal, and their objection would not interfere with our ability to settle with the other leasing companies. I made sure they understood that when the money was gone the money was gone—the client would just borrow less on the mortgages if he were unable to settle with these two lenders.*

The second lender objecting to the payout threatened to not only take the equipment from the closed restaurant but to also call the lease on equipment in the original restaurant, even though the payments were up to date.

I have a good time with smart alecks. In this case, I asked them to let us know when they were coming for the equipment in the restaurant that was making their lease payments, and the name of the company that was going to be taking it out. I told them I wanted to hire the same company to install the new replacement equipment which we would purchase with the funds they didn't want to accept for repayment of the bad lease. Although this did not seem to register with the smart aleck himself, it did with their legal department and owner.

This is a good example of how a bad business decision could have been prevented. A lawyer for the Marco brothers would have done more to prevent the cross-collateralizing and the personal guarantees. An accountant would have advised on the viability of this business venture. And a broker would have sent the client directly to the lawyer and accountant before making such loaded decisions.

When I called the leasing broker to ask why he had not advised the client to get a government-backed Small Business Loan for the business, or why he didn't advise the client to get their lawyer involved, his answer was "it was none of my business." Well, know this: "none of my business," really means that had he done so, he wouldn't have made $20,000 in commissions for arranging the leases. He was in it for the money and not his clients' best interests.

The bottom line: *There are no rules and regulations in the leasing business. Some people care more about their bottom line than the welfare of your business and…Always. Get. The. Team. Involved.*

CHAPTER 8

Experience

When starting a business there's always more to learn. And so, the question becomes, "How do you know if you're ready to start a business?" How much knowledge is "enough" to start your business, and where do you get the experience you need?

You can get a university degree or trade school certification or license but still, that's not experience. Just because you have a real estate licence doesn't mean you have experience buying and selling property. Just because you have a degree in education doesn't mean you have the experience needed to teach. And just because you went to culinary school doesn't mean you have what it takes to open and operate a restaurant.

LEARNING ON THE JOB

When I was young my father told me that you get experience from every job you do. At the time, I didn't believe him. What he wanted me to do was get a job at the local grocery store stocking shelves; all I wondered was, "what can I possibly learn by stocking shelves?"

Experience is not earned in school but by putting in time in the real world. In many fields, such as medicine, dentistry, law, the electrical trade, and plumbing, you need an education to learn what to do in the real world; without it, you don't get the degree or license that will allow you to perform in your career of choice. Your real education begins after you have earned the degree and/or license you seek. The real world is the school that will give you the experience you need to succeed.

So, was my father right when he said we collect experience with every job we do? It turns out that stocking shelves can teach us a lot about things we never think about. First, stores demand that a product be shipped in certain sized boxes with the number of items they want in the box (6, 12, 24, etc.). The reason they want the specific numbers of items per box is that they do not want to open a box, use half of its contents, and put the rest in storage. And did you ever wonder why you can buy items for $1 at a cash-and-carry store that will cost $4 dollars at a grocery or big box store? It's not because the product has been damaged, or it's expired. It's because there was a problem with the box containing the 6/12/24 items. Maybe one of the items was leaking. That one leak either sends the entire box back to the distributor or it gets discarded, and a jobber picks the product up either for free or for a fraction of the original wholesale price.

Did you ever wonder why the most popular everyday brands like Heinz Ketchup sit on the bottom shelf and not the top? That's because in a grocery store you pay for shelf space. Heinz Ketchup does not need any help selling ketchup, so they don't pay to be front and center in order to compete with their competition. They know that if you are a ketchup aficionado, then you will only buy Heinz, and if you do not care about ketchup, you will generally buy the least expensive brand.

Stocking shelves teaches many things about being an employee and how you want or don't want to be treated. How to get along with your manager and co-workers. How employees try to get away with things like longer breaks or doing their job at a slower pace. You'll spot the ones who work harder and spot the ones who are just going through the motions, waiting for the day to end.

These experiences accumulate; you take what you learn with you into the next job or business you own. Experience is everything and it's available for you to learn by watching others or, better still, by asking questions. Just because it's not your job does not mean you can't ask questions about the jobs of other people you work with. Most people are very happy to tell you what their job and responsibilities are.

When I was 20, one of my first jobs, was a three-month summer job as a Boy Friday—basically doing everything— with a mail order business which paid me a whopping $4 an hour plus mileage when I had to drive somewhere.

Day One's lesson came while I was driving with my boss to our only client, American Express. He said, "so you want to be in business? Let me give you your first lesson. Never have a partner." I was surprised.

"But you have a partner," I said.

"Yes, I do," he replied, and then insisted, "Remember what I'm telling you: Never take on a partner who does what you do." One month later he bought his partner out of the business.

Here's what I learned during my first three months of getting paid to go to "business school:"

1. How to determine our product's cost.
2. How large the mark-up is in the mail order business.
3. How jewelry is marked-up.
4. How to clear items at customs without a broker.
5. How to be quick on my feet.
6. How to deal with the post office.
7. Packaging.
8. Dealing with returns or problems.
9. Making sure you do not lower your price on the promise of larger orders in the future.

These are things that will take you far and they are not taught in school.

Generally, the mark-up in the mail order business is at least three or four times the cost. If you pay attention to the TV ads offering you a product, for, say, $19.99 you will notice that they all state "plus shipping and handling." The shipping and handling generally covers the cost of the product plus the shipping and handling and the profit is the $19.99 charged for the item itself.

When they offer you a second product for free if you just pay the shipping and handling, they are covering all their costs in the shipping and handling. They may even be making a small profit on the shipping and handling. Our costs for jewelry products at the mail order business were easy to determine. We were buying a finished product, so we did not have to worry about the costs of materials, equipment, or labor, however, I did have to determine the other costs in the business in order to determine the jewelry's overall cost to us. The other expenses included promotional mailing and post office fees, a commission to American Express, office overhead (insurance, salaries, and rent), plus anything else you can think of. And then, you add the famous 10% for "who knows what." With the jewelry items we were selling, the fluctuation in gold costs could be a very large problem for us, as we had no ability to raise our prices if the cost of gold went up.

For the items we brought in from outside the country we added: exchange rate, duties, taxes, transportation insurance, packaging, all the expenses listed above, and the 10% for who knows what.

By the way, every expense is rounded up, never down.

CLEARING GOODS AT CUSTOMS

As we moved away from jewelry and into clocks, letter openers, golf clubs, etc., we started to bring in items from other countries, which meant we needed to clear the goods at customs when they came in. Turns out that paying me $4 an hour plus mileage was a lot less expensive than hiring a customs broker. And this is how I learned about clearing goods at customs. It's a very simple process. You go to the customs office where your goods are being held and present the customs agent with the required documentation. The agent will give you a customs form to fill out (in those days you could even get the customs agent to fill it out, although I'm not sure if you still can). You fill out the form, they check the goods, and if they agree to clear them, you pay the duties and/or taxes and take the product with you. It's very simple and a lot quicker and less expensive than using a customs broker.

A Mail Order Promotional Idea

About a year after leaving my job with the mail order business I went to work for a family friend in a recreational real estate mail order business. His business was focused on selling hunting and fishing properties, mostly in Northern Ontario. It was here that I learned about a great mail order promotional idea the company offered only to customers who had purchased a property. Here's how it worked: when we sent people the deed to their property we included a

15% discount coupon—which cost about 1-2 cents per coupon—for any other property they purchased from us. The discount offer was transferable to anyone who wanted to buy a property. If the customer already trusts your business, why not give them an incentive to buy again?

I also learned how to get 15% discounts on advertising in magazines which over the years saved me at least $15,000. Contact me to learn about the advertising discount.

* * * * *

Learning Pays Off

Some years later, when I was in the fur accessory business, I had set up a pop-up retail outlet in New York at the South Street Seaport. Before I left Canada to set up shop, I went to Canadian Customs and presented the goods I was bringing into New York, so if I had to bring any back, I could prove they were from Canada and had not been purchased in the United States. This is something you should do every time you leave your country with goods for business. This way customs has a record that you took the goods down and did not buy them in whichever country you were showing them for your business.

Business was good and I was continuously shipping goods down—and paying duties, as I should be doing. But eventually winter ended and there's not a big market for fur accessories in the spring and summer seasons. I returned with a suitcase of fur accessories that I obviously ought to declare, and I did. I got a very rude customs agent—although I had never had one before and haven't had one since—who insisted I get a customs broker to clear the goods and pay duties. I showed him the green forms from Canadian Customs I had obtained before I left to make sure this did not happen. He said he didn't care.

This is where my earlier experience with customs came in handy. The first thing I said was, "You will fill out the B13 form (turns out they had not changed the form in seven years) not me and not a customs broker but before you fill it out go get your supervisor and explain why you are not accepting forms from Canada Customs.

The next words out of his mouth were, "Do you sell raccoon earmuffs?"

I answered "Yes."

He asked, "how much?"

I answered "$20." Then he said, "I'll give you $10, to which I said, "deal." I took out a pair of raccoon earmuffs, he took $10 out of his wallet and away I went.

If I had not had the earlier experience, I most likely would have had to hire a customs broker, pay duties I did not owe, and come back to the airport to pick up the goods in the next day or two.

Every job you do—if you're curious and interested in learning from it—will teach you something new that you can use repeatedly throughout your life.

BEING QUICK ON YOUR FEET

Sometimes plans don't go the way you want them to so what should you do? Simple. Change them before you get into trouble.

When we sold products through the American Express mail order business, we had to present the product to the VP of the mail order operations before moving forward with the test run. The presentation goes something like this: You present the product as well as the first draft of the printed promotional piece. They'll either sign off on the product or not. If they sign off on the product, then you move to the printed promotional piece and if any changes are needed, they're made.

During one of our presentations, the product was not precisely the same as the item in the printed promotional piece. The VP didn't seem to care enough to notice but his associate did and started to comment. My boss immediately stopped the presentation of this item and moved onto the next. No excuses, no explanation, no "yeah-buts"…he just moved on.

Many other businessowners would have kept trying to sell the item, would have made up excuses for why the product and picture didn't match exactly. Not smart.

My boss realized he was caught and wasn't about to risk ruining his reputation and quite possibly his relationship with American Express for a single item that didn't matter in the grand scheme of his business. He let it go and moved on to the next big thing.

NEVER LOWER YOUR PRICE ON THE PROMISE OF MORE BUSINESS

In every business that sells products, two things go hand in hand: you want to sell for the highest price and your client wants to pay the lowest price. To have a selling price you need to understand your costs inside and out. Whether you're buying raw materials to produce your product or buying a finished product and selling it to your customer, you want the best price. There are many factors that go into price fluctuations.

Let's discuss this: you obviously want a better price as you buy larger quantities and suppliers are generally good with that. What those quantity levels are will be determined by the products you are buying. You're not going to get a discount for buying 10,000 nails. You might get a discount on 100,000 and you certainly will on 1,000,000. You are not going to get a discount on a printer, but you will on five or 10 printers. So, it does matter what the item is.

As a supplier you must decide what those discount levels are and it's your costs that go into those decisions, i.e., the discounts you can get based on the volume you purchase from your supplier. Then ask this question: As your business grows will you be able to afford to automate? If you are a manufacturer, will you be able to put on a second shift? If you can automate and add a second shift, you'll reduce your costs and therefore your business will be in a better position to provide better prices to your clients without reducing profits. You may say to yourself that automation costs money and a second shift adds to the payroll, and you wouldn't be wrong. To a point. Your out-of-pocket costs went up, but your production costs didn't. Automation is a one-time cost which will allow you to produce more in the same period which—in turn—results in a cost reduction. And while it's true that adding a second shift does add to your payroll, you're only adding the second shift to cover more business. And so, your profits go up with more production per day. Remember, most of your factory overhead remains the same (rent, property taxes, insurance etc.) but now you have a second shift of production. This goes back to understanding all your costs.

LEARN HOW TO COST

There was a new product we wanted to test before doing a full out mailing through American Express. It was a wooden box with a beautiful navy blue velvet inlay, and it held six decorative enamel spoons. I'm no spoon collector but it was a very nice item. We needed to know how to price it, so we asked for a price on 2,000 boxes with the spoons.

The supplier was excited to provide us with a great price on 2,000 boxes. The thing is, we didn't know how many we would need as we had not yet run the test mailout to 10% of American Express cardholders. We only ordered 50. We needed the product on hand before doing the mailout as this was part of the conditions of selling through American Express and 50 was the minimum we would need to sell to determine if this was a product to go to a full mailout or not.

Turns out we did not hit 50 sales number and the full mail out was cancelled.

So back to the manufacturer who was waiting on the delivery date for the remaining 1,950 boxes. But we never gave him an order, we had only asked for a price on 2,000. He understood differently, thinking that we ordered 2,000 and he ordered all the materials to fulfill that quantity. What he should have done was given us a price for 50 units and another price for the remaining 1,950 units. There was nothing underhanded; just a manufacturer hearing what he wanted to hear. He had a second opportunity to correct his position when he got the order for the first 50. He should have asked about the other 1,950. He should have asked for a hard purchase order from us. I promise you he never made this mistake again. Had I not learned this lesson, my business trip to the Philippines a year later would have ended up costing me a lot of money. Thanks to a connection through a friend's father, I went to the Philippines to look for products to import and resell. One of the products I found was a sportswear clothing line. Another friend's brother and their father were planning to open a new bakery chain in the very near future. I got in front of the father with my sporty polo shirts and showed him all the different color combinations available to see if any of them worked for the uniforms for his new bakery chain. One was exactly the colors of his brand and I mean exactly. Ralph Lauren himself could not have come closer to the colors they had picked out. He asked for a price on 300 shirts, and I told him it would be $14.50/each. He then asked me to order 30 to which I said "okay, but for 30 the price is $17.50/each."

"You just said $14.50," he said.

"Yes, that's correct for 300," I said. "But you only want 30, and my costs are higher for that, so I need to charge $17.50. But here's what I will do for you. I'll charge $17.50 on the 30 you're ordering now and when you place the order for the other 270, I will charge $14.50 and rebate the extra $90 you paid on the first 30. This gets you back to the $14.50 price that I quoted for 300."

He said "no." I thanked him for the opportunity but would not be able to supply him. Had I not seen what had happened to the box manufacturer, I probably would have agreed to his request for 30 shirts at $14.50, excited that another 270 would be ordered.

This was a good lesson on recognizing the people you don't want to do business with. This was a wealthy man who was given a fair deal. His son was my friend, and he had known my mother for many years. It was impossible to deny that my shirt was a perfect 100% match to the colors of his new business and still, he was trying to beat me for $90. This is the kind of person you never want to do business with. This is the kind of person who has it in him to order the other 270 shirts and when they come in, offer less than the $14.50 or threaten to cancel the order if I didn't agree to the reduction.

The moral of the story; if you're fair and the other side isn't, run as fast as you can and look for business somewhere else. No matter how big the order, trouble will find you when dealing with people like this.

THE COST OF DOING BUSINESS, FROM A MAIL ORDER PERSPECTIVE

How you deliver your product is crucial to your success. Sometimes it's about pricing and sometimes it's about convenience. In the mail order business, it is crucial to get your product out as soon as you get the order. You want your customer to get that product while they are still very excited that they ordered it.

So, how do you determine who you use to deliver the item? First you must decide what you want as proof of delivery. Do you want the purchaser to have to go to the post office to pick-up the item (not really a great idea), do you want the purchaser to sign for the product when it is delivered (that's a problem if no one is home), or are you okay with the item just being left at the person's door?

The decision as to whether you want someone to sign for the product will most likely be based on the value of the item. Having someone sign for the item makes the delivery more expensive and harder to deliver since someone must be home. If you are okay with the delivery company just dropping it off, then the delivery costs are going to be lower because the item is easier to deliver. So, basically, the decision to make is, "do I want to go into the insurance business or not?" because essentially, this is what you're doing. You're either paying a higher delivery charge to have someone sign for the item or you are the insurance company hoping the item is not stolen or the client says they didn't get it when they did.

If that doesn't work for you, your choices are the post office or a delivery service. For me, the answer was convenience, and, in my situation, it saved money as well. I chose a delivery service over the post office. With the delivery service I had to call them "today" for a pickup "tomorrow" for a delivery the next day. I also did not have to be home when they came to pick up the packages, I was able to leave the items in my garage for pickup. This was basically a three-day delivery. The alternative was the post office but with the post office, I had to go there, wait in line, and pay extra with no guarantee the product would get there the next day. I was too busy—and one extra day for delivery was no problem, especially when the post office was not willing to guarantee next day delivery, even though they were charging a premium.

When I worked for the mail order business, we used the post office because of the value of the items. The people were friendly, and going there got me out of the office, but this was still the post office with very stringent rules. Plus, they can go on strike anytime and trust me, the headaches are real when that happens.

DEALING WITH RETURNS

In the mail order business, we did not deal with very many returns. A lot of the items were for gifts, so they did not come back and if they did it was for a size or color exchange. Since we got the order out so quickly, the customer was still excited to get their package, and so we did not get returns due to people changing their minds.

The returns we got were not extraordinary or excessive and therefore we just accepted them as part of doing business. But how do you protect against large volume returns? Sell a good product and deliver when promised. Those two company policies will eliminate almost all your returns. Keep track of who returns to you. Occasionally you will have the same person ordering and returning. If that happens do not take their orders in the future. Department stores now keep track of all returns and will flag customers that regularly return items. You can do the same.

One of my customers in the fur accessory business returned two pairs of rabbit earmuffs which sold for $6 each. Her reason for the return was that they were not the blue she had ordered. By the way, her return was packaged with another return for another company which led me to think she was a chronic returner of products that did not sell in her store. Another clue: there was only one color of blue rabbit fur in the entire country, and it was brought into the country by only one fur dealer. There was no chance that she had seen any other blue rabbit color. One other thing: I was the only person in Canada who sold colored rabbit earmuffs. Returns are a pain to deal with and end up costing you money.

If you are selling to big box stores let them know that you have a policy of no returns for credit. You will only provide replacements for damaged goods at your expense. This policy ensures that you do not get returns for products that do not sell fast enough in the store.

LESSON LEARNED: NO RETURNS

One of my factoring clients taught me this one. She had been a buyer at Sears and later she started selling a product to Sears. Her policy was simple: if an item was broken, she would pick up the broken item and deliver a replacement at her cost. But she would not allow other returns. She showed me the returns she got from Sears, and they amounted to a whole four items out of a 30,000-piece order. At $10 each, that came to a $300,000 sale. Genius. That taught me to never factor an invoice from a retail chain unless there was a no-return policy in the contract.

Today a lot of retail chains accept returns and damaged goods and simply discount each invoice by 1-3%. If returns amount to less than the 1-3% allotted, then the store wins; if they are greater than that, then they will increase the discount the next year, or they may stop purchasing that item from you.

Stand behind your product, honor your warranties, respond to your customers' calls immediately and you will have fewer problems.

LEARNING YOUR BUSINESS LESSONS

When I started working in the factoring business, I told myself that I'd either be buying into the factoring business, starting my own factoring company, or buying into one of the clients' businesses. Now it was time to go to school and get paid for it. Although this factoring business was two years old when I went to work there, it was really a new business as during the first two years they only factored car insurance claims and I had no interest in that area of the business. So, we started a new division for B2B businesses. We gave our first client a $10,000 limit and lost $25,000. After the first step backwards, the business took off. The next client I signed up made the business and put in place a lot of the protocols the business would need to grow successfully. With my goal of buying or starting my own factoring company, I was asking everyone what their responsibilities were and in time I understood everyone's job.

As I acquired new knowledge about their jobs and how the business financed itself, I was able to come up with new ideas on factoring receivables that did not sit inside the factoring box.

I had a friend who was very interested in buying a franchise restaurant. He knew how to eat; however, he did not know how to cook. He knew how to work hard, however, he knew nothing about the restaurant business. So, before investing $500,000 in the franchise he went to school.

He took a job at a large family restaurant as a bus boy. Then he worked in the kitchen washing dishes. Eventually, he got to prep food and, finally, to cook. From there, he came out from the hot kitchen and became a host. From hosting, he started to bartend and finally started working as a waiter.

His friends asked him why he was working in a restaurant for such little pay, and this is where I heard for the first time the saying "I'm getting paid to go to school." Which is exactly what he was doing and after six months or so he bought the franchise and became the highest grossing first year franchisee for that chain; by the second year, he was the top franchisee.

His work ethic and determination had not been in question, but his lack of experience was. He was determined to buy the franchise, so he got the experience which gave him the confidence to purchase the franchise. Always be learning.

CHAPTER 9

Leaving Your Job

I get asked one particular question a lot, and you're probably wondering this, too: "When should I leave my current job to start my new business?" The answer to this question is different for everybody as it depends on each person's unique situation. To answer this question, you need to have a discussion with your family. You need to prepare everyone for a tightened budget as you start out on your new venture. You'll want to resolve how the bills will get paid and, if you have a working spouse, how much of your personal monthly obligations he or she will contribute to the monthly expenses and what will be left for you to pay. With a family, there is a lot more planning involved and the timing on leaving your job is a very important family decision.

If you happen to be single with only yourself to consider, then you have an obvious advantage with more options. You might be able to live with a family member, take a roommate to split living expenses, or downsize your living space to save money while getting your business off the ground.

Another thing—are you leaving to start a business that will compete with your present employer? If you are, keep it quiet. Never discuss your new business with any of your current work colleagues. If you're thinking of asking any of them to join you in your new venture, wait until after you have left and have started your new business. If you're not leaving to compete and you have a good relationship with your employer, then you can and probably even *should* discuss your new business with your employer. Maybe there is a way for you to work part-time before you leave for good. If that's not an option, then hold off as long as possible before discussing your new business and giving notice.

The decision to leave will hopefully be yours. You should investigate what unemployment options there might be for a person starting their own business. You might qualify for what is referred to as an entrepreneurial unemployment. You might have to be laid off from your job to qualify, so it's best to check with an unemployment office sooner rather than later as the rules change all the time.

ASK ABOUT ENTREPRENEURIAL UNEMPLOYMENT INSURANCE

When you go into the unemployment office to get information, make sure you stipulate that you are starting your own business and do not expect to be able to draw any salary for some time.

When I started a new business, I applied for unemployment insurance, thinking, "Why not? I've paid into the system for so many years, and I won't be drawing a salary for some time." I got the unemployment insurance for the first four months of my new business and stopped taking it as soon as I started to take a salary.

About a year after stopping the unemployment, I received a call from someone from the unemployment department who wanted to meet with me. A woman arrived at my office and asked me why I had three employment remittances for the previous year. One from my old employer, the second from the unemployment office and the third from my new business. Well, the one from my former employer was an estimation of what I still had coming to me in the form of commission and was not a severance package. That was okay with the unemployment officer.

The third one from my business was also "okay" with the unemployment officer.

However, the one from the unemployment office was not okay. She wanted to know why I didn't apply for entrepreneurial unemployment insurance, to which I had to ask, "what is entrepreneurial unemployment insurance?" Who knew there was such a thing as an unemployment package for entrepreneurs? So, I asked her about the qualifications, and it turns out they're the same as regular unemployment. You qualify for the same amount and for the same period. If you worked in the same industry as the business you started, then you do not need to do anything else but apply. If you start a business where you cannot prove you have experience, then you might have to take a week of training. However, you must apply specifically for entrepreneurial unemployment insurance in order to get it.

When I told her I had never heard of entrepreneurial unemployment benefits before, her answer was that "I should have looked for the pamphlets at the unemployment center." Maybe this is a government-issued secret because 30 years later I have yet to meet a single person who has ever heard of entrepreneurial unemployment.

Turns out that I had to pay back all the unemployment I had received for four months plus a 50% penalty because I would have qualified for the entrepreneurial unemployment but didn't sign up for it. I did not, however, need to pay back the unemployment with a 100% penalty because I did not commit fraud by continuing to take the unemployment after I started to earn a salary from my business. Lucky me.

I'm sure I could have fought this and won, but it just was not worth it at the time. So, make sure you go to your unemployment office and get all the information you need about how you qualify for the unemployment insurance… before you need it.

STARTING A BUSINESS THAT COMPETES WITH YOUR FORMER EMPLOYER

When do you leave your employer to start a competing business? I suggest leaving as soon as you've made the decision to start the business. The last thing you want to do is warn your employer and give them a reason to make it hard for you. They might cause a financial problem for you if you are due any salary, holiday pay, severance pay, or your record of employment for unemployment benefits or commissions. Best to be out the door long before your employer finds out about your new competing business.

If you signed an employment contract when you started working or during the time you were at your former employer, make sure you take your contract to an employment lawyer to be reviewed. If your contract stipulates that you cannot go after any of the company's clients, that is something you need to review with your employment lawyer. Generally, in your contract there will be either:

1. A condition that you can never solicit the company's clients or

2. 2. A specified time period during which you cannot solicit the company's clients. Your employment lawyer will let you know how long that period is after reading any employment contract you signed.

It cannot be an unreasonable period. No one can stop you from working in any industry, including your previous employer, no matter what you signed, unless you were given a settlement in some form when you left that stipulates what period the settlement package covers. I'm not a lawyer so speak to your employment lawyer about this. Think about it this way: if you're a lawyer or an accountant working for a large firm and you decide to leave to set up your own firm, how can you be stopped from making a living? The same would apply to any industry you worked in.

Now, there might also be a condition in your employment contract stipulating where you might not be able, geographically, to set up your business. This cannot be an unreasonable restriction. Again, go back to your employment lawyer for clarity on this. You cannot take anything from your employer, even if you wrote the software, invented something, etc., because the company has proprietary rights to those items not you, even though you were responsible for them. If you are uncertain, speak to your employment lawyer.

"For All Your Factoring Needs, Call Michael"

When I went to work for a factoring company, they had me sign an employment contract. After reading it I knew that most of it was not enforceable, but to be sure I brought it to a lawyer who also agreed that most of it was not enforceable. The contract said I could not work in the industry for two years from the day I left—which was not enforceable. I could not be denied a livelihood. The second clause stipulated that

I could not open a business within 200 miles of any of the company's clients—which was not enforceable. The third clause said I could not contact any of the company's clients for two years–probably not a fully enforceable time limit.

What no contract could ever do is stop clients from contacting me and so if someone contacted me, I was totally free to do business with them. The factoring company could not stop a client from moving their business over to me. After almost six years of working for the factoring company—entirely on commission, which I had no problem with at all—my clients were mine for as long as they used the factoring company's service. That is, until the day the owner decided to change the policy and stipulate my clients could only be my clients for another 12 months. Furthermore, any new clients I brought in would be mine for only 12 months. I gave him 12 months' notice.

Within six months the owner let every other account manager go, which left just me. I guess he felt he needed me. He offered a different arrangement: to replace the 12-month client limit he put in place just six months earlier. While waiting for his new offer, I met some people who were looking for salespeople to sell viatical settlements—a transaction in which a terminally ill individual sells their life insurance to another party. I heard them out but wasn't interested and explained that I was in the factoring business and wanted to stay in it. One of the people involved in the meeting asked me to explain the factoring business to him. Within three meetings we had a deal outlined to set up a new factoring business. This group would provide the financing and I would provide the expertise. I made sure I did not mention my plans to anyone with whom I was then working.

A month passed and my employer came to me with a new deal. It laid out a salary and outlined a bonus plan but made no mention of any commission. The monthly salary he was prepared to pay me would not cover my personal monthly expenses. The bonuses were to be paid every six months with a cap on each of the four bonus categories. With the conditions imposed on the bonuses, one of the bonuses could not even be earned some years.

Even if I earned 100% of all the bonuses each year plus my salary, I wouldn't make close to what I had earned in the previous two years on straight commission. After a couple of weeks, he called me into his office and asked why I had not signed back the new employment agreement. I said, "I can't afford to work for you under these conditions." Within a week he informed me that he would like me to leave at the end of the year if I was not going to accept the new arrangements. I said, "not a problem. Write me a check." He asked, "how much" and I said, "you write it and if my brothers—both lawyers—say it's enough, fine with me. If not, you'll have to write a bigger check.

He offered me more than what I was willing to accept, and I accepted it under one condition: he had to pay me on January 2, instead of December 31. I didn't want to pay income tax on the commission settlement in a year when I had made money, especially when I didn't know when I would be able to take a salary from my new business. He had no problem paying me in January, we left on good terms and things remained that way for about two months. At that point the factoring company's largest client contacted me to see if I'd provide a larger limit than the one they had had with my former employer.

I knew this about the client: they had helped build my former employer's factoring company and if they moved over to mine, they would likewise help me build it. I went to my partners and told them that if we took on this client, we would instantly be profitable, however, there might be a large fight coming our way with the other factoring company. My new partners were lawyers. They reviewed my employment agreement and felt there was no problem whatsoever with accepting this client or any other former clients that contacted me. So, we raised the money to buy the client out of his factoring arrangement with my former employer.

The client, my partner, and I went to the factoring company with a bank draft in hand to pay off the account. When the owner came out of a meeting and saw us, he demanded to know why we were there. The client suggested we wait for him in the parking lot while he discussed things with my former employer. Five minutes later, after paying off his now-former factoring company (my former employer) my first new client said, "I hope when we finish doing business together, we can shake hands and thank each other."

Apparently, the owner of the factoring company was extremely upset that not only was he getting paid off and losing the account, but he was losing the account to me.

Everyone loses clients, that's just part of doing business. How you handle the loss speaks volumes about you and your business. Always thank your client and wish them the best. You never know—they may come back or refer other clients to you, but neither will happen if you are disrespectful to them.

One of the first rules that my former employer taught me about the factoring business was that you never let a client get away with taking your money without going after them full tilt, even if it costs you money you'll never get back. You need to make sure other clients know that no one gets away with stealing your money. Which was ironic given what happened next.

When you buy an existing account from another factoring company there most likely will be a few invoices in the first week or two after the account is moved that belong to the new factoring company but were sent to the old factoring company by mistake. These payments now belong to the new factoring company, and it's the old factoring company's responsibility to call the new one to let them know that they received payment on an invoice or invoices not belonging to them. It is then up to the new factoring company to make arrangements to collect these funds from the old factoring company.

Well, that's the way it's supposed to go. Just one day after the account was paid, the former company received a check in the mail that now belonged to us...but they refused to hand it over. That constitutes theft. Going by my former employer's rules, i.e., "never let anyone get away with taking your money," I went nuts. My partners—being lawyers—said they'd back me up and go after him for taking the check that belonged to us, however, lawsuits are expensive and time consuming. Maybe there was a better way. They were prepared to back me all the way, but first, they wanted to try resolving the problem directly with the factoring company. Who was I to disagree?

They succeeded in getting the factoring company to forward $18,000 of the $33,000 they had received. What's more, the settlement they negotiated included a clause that said that any other checks were to be turned over in full immediately, that the employment contract I signed was null and void, and that I could now go after any clients that had been mine at my former employer's factoring company. What I did next was immature, and a total waste of time, energy, and money so, no matter how much you will want to, don't do what I did next.

My partners and my brothers tried to stop me, but I couldn't swallow the fact that my former employer took a check that didn't belong to him and made me pay to get it back. I couldn't let it go so I decided to put a bench sign (a paid advertisement) across the road from his office that he would have to see each day when he left work. The bench sign read "For all your factoring needs call Michael Yasny." The after-noon the bench sign was placed, I got a call from a former colleague letting me know the message had been received, loud and clear.

A couple of months later I had the sign removed and placed in another location for the remainder of the 12-month contract. Was it worthwhile to me? I have to say, yes, it was. Did it accomplish anything other than make me feel good for a day and have a story to tell? No. It was a waste of time and money—I never got a client from either location.

CHAPTER 10

Your Business Plan and Your Marketing Efforts

DO I REALLY NEED A BUSINESS PLAN? THE ANSWER IS "YES" AND "NO"

In essence, a business plan tells a story about what your business is about—your costs, the financing you need, the clients you are hoping to get, and the competition you will face. A business plan will show clearly how much or how little you understand about your business and it's a great way to introduce potential lenders and partners to your new or growing business.

I have never read a business plan that showed the business was going to operate at a loss and yet, once you open your business, the plan tends to not even be relevant. Banks and lenders like to see a plan, but I do not know any lenders—I'm not talking about family and friends here—who would actually lend you any money based on what they see in your business plan. This is not to say you shouldn't write one. It's an excellent exercise in helping you understand the business you are intending to run.

Get your accountant to help with the business plan by either overseeing your writing of the plan or by referring you to a person who writes business plans for a living. If you have not written more than one business plan in your career, then you are probably not the right person to write this one. The accountant or professional business plan writer will have a much better understanding of what goes into a plan and what should be left out, but they will need your input.

MARKETING YOUR BUSINESS

Part of your business plan is a marketing plan. We all need to market our business to attract clients but what kind of marketing should you undertake? Let's start with what kind of marketing is available. Advertising is the first thing everyone thinks of when looking at marketing their business. It's also generally the most expensive form of marketing. There are other marketing tools available:

- Door to door sales works and you usually pay—a commission—only if the salesperson is successful
- Cold calling works but it's tough and everyone hates it
- Dropping off flyers and business cards is basically a hope-and-pray marketing method

Social media is a great option, but which platforms will work best for your new business? Social media marketing is an expense that can take six-to-twelve months to run its course, so you need to understand the costs and you need patience to see things through. If you are not financially prepared to see it through, then don't even start as you will just be wasting your limited marketing budget.

Networking is an inexpensive and interactive way to get your business name out there. You just need to try different networking venues to find out which networking groups are best for your business. Through networking you are going to meet people who are in the marketing business. Get them to give you proposals (they don't cost anything). However, make sure they understand your business. Many of these companies say they can help but if they do not understand your business, how can they put a marketing plan together that is going to work for your business?

Part of marketing is about making sure you have the right kind of website, logo, and catchphrase for your business. Marketing companies can help with any or all of these. However, be leery of companies that say they do everything, and that they're the best at all of it. Get referrals, ask to see case studies, find out what they did in each case. A company someone refers you to will be friendly to them, so ask questions that relate to what you are seeking. Find out if they are still doing business with that marketing company and if they are not, why not.

Marketing companies must do their own marketing research on businesses they approach. If they approach without having an idea about what their client cares about, what their values and philosophy are, what does this say about them? This was a lesson I had to learn myself when I applied for a job and the person interviewing me asked me what I knew about their business. Nothing. All I knew was that they were a commercial real estate brokerage. I didn't check them out. Not a good start. If marketing companies pitch to you without taking the time to learn about your business before they call, how good can they possibly be at what they do?

I've had many marketing companies approach me after seeing some form of advertising from me. They all wanted to help me and knew they would do a great job. Here are the first two questions I asked: *Do you know what I do, and do you understand my business?* I do not remember one single company being able to answer yes to both those questions. Most of the time, if not every time, they had no idea what kind of financing I did, and they had absolutely no understanding of my business. When I asked how much they charged, amazingly almost everyone said $3,000.

When I said, "You say you know how to help me and you're confident you can, but how do I know that you'll be successful?" The answer was generally the same, "We are very good, and very successful helping our clients."

This is the tester I would use with these companies because I believe in doing business this way. Most of the fees I charge are based on my success. Yes, sometimes I charge some of or all my fees upfront but in general, 80%

of the fees I charge to help finance a business come from success. I believe in betting on myself.

Suggestions for Dealing with Marketing Companies

Clients are more likely to accept higher fees when fees are tied to successful outcomes

This is a strategy I've used more than once. *With one marketing company representative I said, "Okay, so your fee is $3,000 and you tell me you are always successful. So, how about I pay you $6,000 but only if you are successful?" I even offered someone $9,000 but, again, only if they were successful. The answer was always the same, "NO." I never hired any of them.*

I did find two women to take me up on my offer for another business I owned. At first, they were not prepared to accept our offer of getting paid only on success. Eventually, they took a chance (they had nothing else going on) and ended up earning three times the amount they wanted us to pay. They did very well, and we did very well. That was a win-win situation, which is what everyone is looking for in business.

An Adage to Apply Throughout Your Business

If it sounds too good to be true, it is. I met a person who spoke at a networking event that I attended. I thought what he was offering was something that would work for my business. He said he'd be able to get me to first place on Google for a reasonable setup fee and a small monthly fee to keep me there. It worked but there was a catch—aside from the monthly fee to keep me in first place, the searcher had to type in a very specific question which brought them to a question-and-answer statement I had made. If the searcher didn't type in the exact question, they would not be able to find or contact me. This turned out to be not only a complete waste of my money but also my time.

Be Very Cautious with Monthly Marketing Programs

The next lesson to learn just makes me laugh. The same individual came to me with the next round of marketing. He had someone who would be able to help market my company on Facebook. I was seeking help, so I was open to setting up a meeting. He presented me with a full, glossy, bells-and-whistle slideshow over breakfast. The last slide was their offer: A six-month program of $1,800 a month to manage up to $400 in Facebook advertising. After I stopped laughing, I bombarded them with what I thought to be fair and intelligent questions that any prospective client should ask. First and most importantly, I wanted to know what they do for $1,800 a month (which was 4.5 times my advertising budget). To which they answered that they monitor advertising 24 hours a day. Well… don't you have other clients? Do you have any real idea what I do? Does your staff understand what I do? How can you spend that much time on *one account and what exactly are you monitoring 24 hours a day? I obviously did not engage their services.*

People are hungry. People want (need) your business. People will try to lure you in.

These people tried to overcharge on the first offer. The next day they came back with an offer to lower their $1,800 to $1,100 a month. You can guarantee the second offer was still an overcharge. Any business that can reduce their fees by almost 40% in a single day for a new client is not someone to have another conversation with. I offered them an unlimited commission on all the business their advertising on Facebook brought me. This offer would have earned them 2-10X more in commission than the $1,800 per month they wanted to charge. They turned it down.

They took me for a sucker instead of a client that could be with them for years. I have never used the first guy for anything else, and I have never referred any business to him. If anyone ever did contact me, I would do my best to make sure they did not do business with this person or his company. I guess that is why he has never used me as a referral.

CHAPTER 11

Hiring, Delegating, and Being the President

Eventually you will need employees for your business. You might need them the first day you open your business or down the road as your business grows. The right employee can make your business and the wrong employee will cost you clients and possibly ruin your business. You must spend the necessary time to hire the best employee for each position, and financial compensation should be the last and least important part of the hiring process.

HOW TO HIRE

You should not hire an employee until you can't physically do the job you want the employee to do. When you hire people to do jobs you have time to do yourself, that's when you start to waste valuable money. This is money you can use later to pay that new employee. There will be jobs that you have the time to do but don't want to do, and you must get the idea out of your head that you are the president, and the job is beneath you. You must do the job no matter how much you hate it until you really can't anymore (unless there are physical limitations), and then you can spend the money on an employee to do that job. You will have no choice but to hire someone if you have a job in your business that needs special training or a license you do not have. The valuable money you saved by doing the jobs you hated is now available to pay the new employee without damaging your cash flow position. Call the money you saved doing the job yourself a loan to the company that you never have to pay back.

When I started my first business (the fur accessory business) I gave myself a wonderful $2,000 lesson. I had a very menial job that had to be done and instead of doing it myself I decided to hire two young guys to do it. Hey, why should I do it? I was the "President" and I had sports to watch on TV.

I ended up having to do 90% of the job over again and became $2,000 poorer. This turned out to be a very expensive lesson then, but a lucrative one going forward as I have followed the rule to this day, that you do everything yourself until you can't possibly do it; then you hire someone.

When I started the retail part of my fur accessory business, I had to be open seven days a week, so there was no choice but to hire someone to work during the week. I had the business to run—which was producing the product for my wholesale and retail business—so there was no way I could handle everything. However, I was at the retail store every Saturday, Sunday, and holiday.

This was a minimum wage job so how did I manage to get responsible employees to work for me? I paid more than everyone else. Minimum wage was $4 an hour and I paid $6. That is 50% more than everyone else was paying their employees, which cost me $110 more a week than everyone else. And I would do it again. This was money well spent because I made more money by producing the product than by selling a small number of items during the week. By paying 50% more than everyone else I attracted better and more responsible employees.

About three or four months after I started my own financial business, I hired my first secretary. She fit all the boxes: she was married, middle-aged, had teenage children, needed the job, had a solid, confirmed reference from her past employer, and she was happy with the salary I was offering.

Sounds perfect, right? She lasted a week. The job took up no more than three hours on a busy day and she was paid for the entire day. Turns out the job was too complicated for her. This job could have successfully been handled by a smart 10-year-old or a not-so-smart 12-year-old. I went to my partners and asked what I should do? They suggested I give her a week's notice and let her go. I said we couldn't afford to have her there that long. I sat her down and explained that I did not think things were working out and that I had to let her go but I would give her a second week's pay. You never saw a person so relieved to be fired in your life.

I would go on to have six secretaries over the next 12 years. I did not hire one of them. I realized that the best person to hire a female employee was another woman and after the first hiring failed after only a week, I knew I had no idea what I was doing. So, I let women do the hiring for me. Sometimes it was the secretary leaving who helped hire her replacement, sometimes it was an employee from my partner's business who did the interviewing and once it was an employment agency. Out of six secretaries, I only let one go. That's not to say I wasn't involved in the hiring. I would meet with them first to give them a brief idea of what the job entailed and then introduce them to the person who would be conducting the interview. After the interview process, the interviewer would give me their opinion on the best candidates and then the three of us would meet again. The final decision came down to who was going to be the happiest getting the job, and what could I do to make them happy, so I did not have to go through this again anytime soon.

One candidate wanted to leave at 4:00 p.m. instead of 5:00 p.m. This was no problem. Even though the job now took longer than three hours a day it was still not an eight-hour-a-day job, so leaving at 4:00 instead of 5:00 did not make any difference whatsoever. I wound up with a responsible, organized secretary who stayed with me for three years.

Another candidate had had a very bad experience with her previous employer because she needed to see an allergist once every two weeks for a shot to help with her severe allergies. They made her fill out requests to do this and always gave her a hard time. The two women who did the interviewing really liked this woman even though she seemed very shy. I took a liking to her and offered her the job at a couple of thousand dollars less for a three-month probation period and told her she would get a raise over what she was making after that. I threw in another condition: every two weeks when she had to see her allergist, I wanted her to go in the morning before work. She did not need to ask permission, but I asked her to just please go in the morning. I wound up with the best employee imaginable. She was punctual, grateful, hardworking, and never left before 5:30 in a job that required her to stay only till 5:00.

One suggestion: never hire someone for less money than they were earning before. After my first secretary was let go, one of the candidates to replace her was prepared to take the job at $30,000 even though she had been earning $40,000 at her old job and had asked for $40,000. This was a red flag for me. That person would never be happy earning 25% less and would always be looking for another job that paid her more.

Also, employees want to be appreciated. They want to feel they are contributing to the success of the business. I've always tried to make sure they felt they were part of the success of the business by involving them in finding ways to make the company better. When I owned part of a manufacturing business, I made sure that anyone who brought forward an idea that was implemented would be rewarded for their suggestion. The reward was generally two-to-four times their weekly take home pay. Your front-line workers will see opportunities for improvement more readily than management. And these improvements could benefit the company by tens of thousands, hundreds of thousands, or even millions of dollars over many years. This is something that is certainly worth rewarding.

Most businesses have large marketing budgets making up a significant percentage of their gross revenue as they try to attract and keep clients. However, it takes only one bad five-minute call between your client and someone at your business to lose that client forever and you will never know why unless you have a policy in place to follow-up with clients who leave your business. You will not only have lost a client without knowing why but they will tell everyone they had a bad experience and left you. People don't spend anywhere as much time telling friends about resolutions to their problem as they do about a problem they had with your business.

How many times have you called your phone company, credit card company or other service provider with a problem only to be treated rudely and not gotten your problem resolved? All of us have been in that position and many of us have moved our business without the company knowing why.

If you are a service provider, it will generally be the employees who earn the least who will cost you the most clients. The less employees have to lose (in terms of income), the less they care. No matter how small or large your business is or becomes, you need to have a customer retention policy, one that follows the acquiring of clients and the loss of clients. This is the only way to determine why you are losing clients.

Don't be afraid to pay the best employees the most. You do not have to hire them at the highest salary but recognize and reward them. Don't wait for them to ask for a raise. If they have to ask, they are probably already looking, they have found something else, or they will be looking shortly. Once they get another job it is generally too late to keep them. They do say "good help is hard to find" and it's true.

When I worked for the factoring company, the owner didn't think his salespeople were important because he valued education over hard work and experience. He never really thought that his sales staff were that important and he figured all of them could be easily replaced. He even cut a top salesperson's territory—not because the guy couldn't handle it, he just didn't think someone with a background as a waiter should be making six figures. There was no other reason.

If you have salespeople, provide them with opportunities that make it possible for them to be the highest earning employees in your business. They are the engine that runs the business because without sales, you have no business. Be a good and respectful employer, be nice to the people you hire, and pay them well and you will be successful, happy, and have few employee problems.

MAKE SURE YOU DELEGATE

Trust your employees to do their job. If you do this properly, your employee might just look at their job as their own little business inside a larger business. The more successful they feel they are the more successful your business will become.

Being able to trust your employees goes back to spending the time to hire the right people for the job. As your business grows you will have less time to oversee every employee every minute of the day. You need to be able to count on your management staff to watch over the employees in their division. Those management staff members need to know that you have confidence in them to make decisions and the only time they need to seek your advice is over large changes that are needed in their division. If you cannot trust them to make decisions, you will never have time to run your business and success will never really be yours.

When I was just 16 or so there was a guy a couple of years older than me who had set up a business installing and repairing TV converters. His business was flying. He was working 12-18 hours a day seven days a week and so, one day, he finally hired a salesperson and someone to help with the repairs. One was a friend and the other a relative. Problem was, he couldn't delegate or trust these employees so instead of spending the time these two new employees freed for him to grow his business, he spent that time micromanaging everything they did. Instead of his business growing it became less profitable because he was now paying the two employees he had hired to help grow his business.

He couldn't grow his business because he could not delegate or trust. This guy always made a living but never became the very wealthy person he should have become.

BEING THE PRESIDENT

Being the president of a company is easy. Order the business cards and emboss "President" under your name. There. Done. Being respected as the leader that you, as president, want to be, that's another thing entirely. The title of President is nothing more than a title. *Being* a president takes dedication. You must be a leader and a teacher. You must be prepared to work harder and longer than any employee in your business. You should be able to fill in for almost every job—if not every job—in your business. Be a person who everyone can come to for anything, without fear. Know how to delegate. You want your employees to see you as a successful, respected person. Sometimes, your employees will come to you with a personal problem rather than a business one. And they will look to you for help with their personal problem when they have no other person to turn to. Listen to them and help them when you can.

A president is a strong person, a good person, and a respected person. Are you that person? If you are, then you are a president, and it does not need to be written on your business card for everyone to know.

CHAPTER 12

Making Sales and Generating Profits

The sales department is the driving force behind every company's success. Without sales, there is no revenue and therefore no business. Where do the sales come from? The first sale is from you, the owner. Your first sale is selling yourself on your product or service. If you do not believe in your product or service more than anyone else, how will you be able to sell it to your clients and then to your employees? You are the number one salesperson in your business, even if you never go on the road to sell your product or service to any potential clients.

Your employees must believe in you in order to be successful. When they believe in you, they will be able to easily relay their belief in the product or service your company is offering to your potential clients.

SALES

Selling is easy. Selling to the right customers at the right price is not so easy. There is a saying that goes: "Sometimes you make more money saying 'no' to a sale than saying 'yes.'" I'm not sure if I made up this saying or heard it somewhere else, but it's so true. What do I mean by that? Well, when you say yes to the wrong sale, problems will come from it. Here's why:

1. If you're paying your employees to produce the order for a "bad sale" then they're not working on sales that will grow your business.

2. A bad sale ties up valuable resources in material, supplier credit, and cash.

3. You may have reduced your price to get the order and are not really making the profit you should.

4. You have a problem getting paid every time. The problems can be a slow payment—which causes you a cash flow problem—extra effort from your staff to try and collect, having to give a discount in order to get paid, having some or all of the goods returned for no good reason, having a problem with your bank because the invoice is overdue, or not getting paid at all, which, depending on the amount, will lead you to writing off the invoice or having to sue, which is expensive. You're paying higher financing charges because it takes too long to get paid or worse, you don't get paid at all.

5. You may miss out on other orders because your cash flow and/or credit with your suppliers is not allowing you to produce orders for your good clients, which could lead to losing those good clients forever.

So, if you had said "no" to that client you would be much further ahead financially.

CREDITWORTHINESS

Strive for *good* sales, not just any sales.

This is where your credit department is so valuable. If you are large enough to have your own credit department, terrific. However, most new companies do not have the financial bandwidth for that, so here's how you can properly assess the creditworthiness of your clients:

1. If you are using a factoring company, they will do this for you in order to protect themselves. They do not want to buy from a company with weak credit. Although your client might not meet the factoring company's credit bar, the factoring company will give you a pretty good idea of the creditworthiness of your client so you can make your own decision.

2. You can use the services of a credit company that insures receivables. They will do a credit check on your client and will either issue credit insurance that limits how much you can sell to them and still be insured, or they won't. Sometimes they will issue a credit limit that is lower than your sale—or combined sales—to the client. Then it is up to you if you want to exceed that limit or not. If you exceed the limit and there is a problem, the insurance company will only pay you up to the limit they established on that client.

3. If you have bank financing and you can arrange receivables insurance, the bank will generally give you a much higher "margining limit," which is like getting a higher limit on your line without your line actually going higher. Most lines of credit have an average margining ratio of 65%, which means that if you have a $650,000 line of credit you need a million dollars in receivables to access the entire $650,000 of your line of credit. If you're able to get credit insurance on your receivables at, say, 90% recovery (the maximum amount the insurance company will pay on any uncollectible invoice), then the bank will generally raise your margining ratio to 90%. So, instead of needing $1,000,000 in receivables to access the $650,000 line of credit you need only have $722,225 in receivables to access the $650,000 line of credit.

4. Sounds great, but not so fast. You're still dealing with an insurance company that will in many cases look for a way to not pay on the claim. There's a way to protect yourself, and if you contact me, we can discuss how to protect yourself from this happening to your business.

INSURANCE

In my 13 years running a factoring company, we took insurance three times and all three times I had to put in a claim on the receivable. The insurance company turned me down every time.

The first two claims were with a credit insurance company overseen by the Federal Government of Canada. In the first claim the insurance company said there was a dispute with the products delivered to my client's client. Because I had protected myself in case this happened I was able to provide immediate proof that there was no dispute and that it just looked like the buyer did not want to pay. The day after I provided the proof, the insurance company said they would pay me.

My client came back to me a second time with the same government insurance for another company and product. This time I took even more precautions. When it was time to get paid, I called the buyer and the very next day after my call, the client closed. I put my claim in with even more proof (although I did not need it since the client went bankrupt) and was paid by the insurance company.

When the client came a third time, I turned down the business because by this time I was sure he was involved with others in a fraud.

Another client came to me with a credit insurance policy from a large credit insurance company owned by a billion-dollar insurance company, which was owned by an even bigger insurance company. Just because it was insured, I took a lot of precautions and protected myself even more carefully, doing even more than if there were no insurance on the invoices (there was no chance I would have bought the invoices if there was no insurance on them). Three shipments were made. One of them was returned and rerouted to another buyer. All shipments and buyers were insured by this credit insurance buyer. I even paid the premiums to make sure they were in good standing.

But you guessed it: all three invoices went bad. I put my claim in and the billion-dollar insurance company said they were not paying. I provided all the proof, including their internal credit report and insurance limit on each buyer. After providing this information and calling the head of claims, the employee's response to me was "F-O." Not sorry, too bad, we aren't paying, just "F-O." I had to sue for the money and only won because I had deep enough pockets to keep fighting. What this shows is that insurance is not always what you think it is. The best use of the insurance is being able to put your bank down as a lost payee on the insurance policy and hopefully this will allow you to get a line of credit, or a large line of credit, or a higher margin against your outstanding invoices.

The credit department, whether it is yours or you pay for it, is part of your sales department. Giving and getting credit is one of the ways your business grows quickly or fails quickly. So be careful when issuing credit.

This is so worth repeating: Sometimes you make more money saying *no* to a sale than saying *yes*.

YOUR CREDIT DEPARTMENT

Your credit department's job is to protect your company and it can also be your sales department's biggest enemy. In fact, the credit department *is* your sales department's biggest enemy. Credit departments protect companies from issuing credit to the wrong companies so in some ways they're lined up with the idea that, "sometimes you make more money saying *no* to a sale than saying *yes*."

Your sales department's job is to bring in sales. The salesperson makes some or all their income from commissions earned on the sales they bring in. If the credit department keeps turning down the sales, the salespeople will look elsewhere for work.

The credit department is set up to protect the company from losing money and yet, ironically, by not extending credit they're losing money and clients for the company. How do you make the credit department a profit center without requiring them to take on any risk or incurring any costs? The answer is purchase order financing, which we discussed earlier in this book. If you can do this, then you will have peace and prosperity between two warring departments.

When the credit department does not want to issue credit to the client, they can introduce them to a Purchase Order Finance company instead of turning the client away. If the POF company is interested in the deal, the credit risk is eliminated. This ends the war between credit and sales, and the profits of the company go up without risk or cost. Every department of your business should be a profit center. Sometimes departments make money for the company, and sometimes they save money; in either situation the company's profits go up.

UNDERSTANDING THE COST OF YOUR PRODUCT OR SERVICE

A lack of understanding around the actual cost of getting your product or service to your clients is a major failure among most new businesses. How can you possibly determine how much you should be selling your product or service for if you do not understand your costs of doing business? Some of your costs —such as rent, insurance, etc.—are fixed and you have them no matter what. Some are almost fixed—like hydro, benefits, office expenses, etc.—and others fluctuate with usage.

HERE'S WHAT GOES INTO YOUR COSTS:

Rent/Mortgage. To determine the cost of occupying your building, divide the rent/mortgage by the number of hours a day you are operating, then by the number of days you are open.

Labor is the cost per shift for hourly workers, office workers, management, and ownership.

Utilities are your gas and hydro and any other utilities you use. Divide the month by the number of days you are operating—if you are closed on the weekends do not count those days—and the number of shifts to get an average; this number is one of the costs that are almost always fixed.

Insurance. This would be for the premises itself, on any financing you have, and any other insurance you pay to insurance companies.

Packaging is the cost of the actual packaging for an individual item—the box it goes in, wrapping, tape, pallets, and dies, if you have special packaging for them.

Shipping is what you pay to bring anything into your location and any shipping costs you must account for to deliver your product to your clients—e.g., your truck, driver, gas, and insurance.

Product warranty and return reserve. Do you offer a warranty on your products? Do you take returns for credit or replacement? This is probably going to be a small percentage of your product or service's final sale cost. What are you budgeting for product problems: 1/100 or 1/1000 pieces? Service calls?

Accounting and bookkeeping. Your accountant is very important at the beginning to help to set your business up correctly with a business plan, a bookkeeping system, and a review of all of your costs. Once things are set up, you will either have an outside bookkeeper taking care of your monthly accounting needs or you will have an internal accounting/bookkeeping department.

Taxes. This refers to any employee taxes to which you must contribute, property taxes if you own the building, and benefits if you offer them.

Income tax reserve. Your accountant will help you with this.

Office expenses. This includes items such as paper, toner/ink, phone-related costs, your copy machine, printers, computers, etc.

Marketing might be one of your biggest expenses. Discuss a budget with your accountant and sales department.

Commission is a percentage that should be added to the production costs of the product or service. It's generally going to be a consistent number based on sales.

Financing costs. This applies to your bank loan or line of credit, leases on equipment, factoring, and any other financing your business uses.

Training. This could be for any training provided to your employees by outside companies. Some of this will be mandatory and some will be for the education and improvement of your employees. You may be able to get some or all of your training expenses re-imbursed by government programs. Have your broker or accountant help determine if you qualify.

Licenses. Does your business or do any of your employees need a license of some kind to keep any designations your business has in good standing?

Exchange rate. Is your business vulnerable to currency exchange through supply purchases or out-of-country sales? Your accountant will help set up a currency reserve.

Commodity protection. If you are dealing with commodities such as metals (copper, zinc, steel etc.) you may want to set up commodity contracts. At the very least you will want to have arrangements in place with your clients for automatic price increases or decreases based on fluctuations in commodity prices.

Duties. These might be charged on products you bring in from other countries.

Custom broker charges for products you bring in from other countries.

Legal expenses. Most businesses have a fixed amount budgeted each month for legal expenses. You may never need to use any or all the reserve but it's best to have it tied into your costs. You never know when you may need to sue a client or defend yourself if one sues you.

Software. Depending on your business you might have minor or major software expenses.

Improvements to your business should be a fixed cost that you have in reserve.

A very important 10% is added last for the "who knows what" unexpected expenses that will pop up. It's your own cost insurance for the unexpected.

Round *up* every expense and never down to build added protection into your products' costs. You never know when you will have to discount your product to sell larger quantities to larger clients.

I have tried to list as many expenses as I can think of but not all of these will apply to your business. You and your accountant must decide which expenses out of this list are appropriate. Some may apply only when you start, and others may only apply years later. This is another area where your team is going to be very valuable to you, especially your accountant and business broker. This is not something you do yourself.

WHAT IF YOUR PRODUCT OR SERVICE IS NOT SELLING?

There could be several reasons for this:

- Did your product/service research show a need for what you're selling?
- Have you identified *which markets* need your product/service?
- Is there a good demand for your product/service?
- Is the marketplace oversaturated with what you offer?

- How many other companies are providing the same service, or is anyone providing that service?

Let's discuss products first. You may think your price is too high and that is why your product is not selling, but it might just be that your price is too low.

PERCEIVED VALUE

Every product has a perceived value. Let's use my fur earmuff business as an example. In general, people perceive products made of real fur to be expensive. That is what is called a perceived value for a product that has nothing to do with what the real costs are. When I was in the fur business, one of the items I sold was a fur headband made from two fox tails. The fur and labor cost me $11, and the headband sold for $29.99. Sales were quite strong. However, several people asked if the headband was made from real fur since the price was so reasonable. They were also comparing the headband price to the fox and mink earmuffs I was selling for $39.99. They could not understand why the headband (which looked so much more expensive) was selling for less than the earmuffs. This was because it cost more to produce the earmuffs than the headband. I didn't know anything about perceived value at the time.

The next year the headband still cost $11 to produce but I raised the price to $39.99 and sold more. The following year I raised the price to $49.99 and sold even more.

People felt better paying more for the product because they perceived fur to be expensive.

Sometimes products do not sell because there is no benefit for a retail store to sell it, even if it is a product that would benefit the public. Sounds strange, doesn't it? The product is something the public could use and would probably buy, but the store does not want to sell it. Why?

What do you think a store's priority is? It's to make money. Their second priority is to make money. And guess what the third priority is? To provide good service to the customer. That's third on the list of priorities. I do not know of any store that will sell products that will cost it money and sales, no matter what the benefit to the customer is.

BIDDING ON LARGE CONTRACTS IS A GOOD WAY TO LOSE MONEY

Years ago, I met, by chance, the vice president (VP) of a large steel company that provided steel to the automotive industry. While we were in conversation, he got an email regarding their latest bid on a GM tender.

So, the story of the tendering goes like this: everyone who wants to bid puts in their offer to sell rolls of steel, and these offers go back and forth for a few weeks. The VP told me they were in first place with their bid. Days later they found out their bid had been beaten and they were asked if they wanted to put in a new offer. They did. And once again they were winning the job. While we were talking, his sales team called to say their bid was now in third place, and they wanted to know what their new bid should be. His answer was fascinating to me.

He told his sales team not to make another bid because they couldn't deliver the entire order—nor could the competition—so they were to let the competition spin their wheels and not make any money. "When they do," he said, "we'll take the leftover business and make money." And that is exactly what happened. They got the bottom part of the order and made money.

You're in business to make money, not to tell everyone who your customers are. If you can't make money with your client, then find others where you can make money, or find a new business.

A STORY ABOUT PAINT CAN LIDS

Here's a great explanation of what it means to focus on selling something that will make you money. I'm pretty sure you have either painted your home or had someone paint it for you. When the painting job was over there probably was a can or two of paint that were not entirely emptied and wound-up in your basement or garage. Then, sometime in the next few years, you needed to do a touch-up and went and got the paint out, only to find that it was either very thick or dried out completely.

I was at the Las Vegas hardware show trying to intro-duce a product I had invented that was designed to be used on wooden fence gates when I met a guy selling a couple of paint products. One of them was a snap on lid for paint cans. It snapped in place on both the inside of the can and the outside. My first thought was, "this guy is going to be very wealthy and how do I get myself involved with him?" I was able to bring my business expertise to the discussion and he brought the product. I thought this was the start of a great partnership. Problem was, he was not looking for a partner, even though we did have many discussions over the next number of years. I took his product to a friend of mine who owns a retail paint store to get his opinion. He thought it was a great product and introduced me to the president of a large paint accessory company. After our initial discussion he introduced me to his righthand man to further discuss this product. Turns out his righthand guy had seen the product in Las Vegas, and even though he liked it he had said, "there's no chance that the big box stores will sell it."

"Why not?" I asked. "If it's such a great product, why wouldn't they want to sell it?" He asked me a question and then everything made sense "What's one of the biggest departments in the big box store?"

I said, "The paint department, and this is a great product to keep the paint fresh." He said "Exactly. And why would they want to keep the paint fresh?"

Now I started looking at it from the store's point of view. They sell a gallon of paint for $40-$80 and the paint can lid would sell for around $5. They make a lot more money selling a gallon of paint than they do selling a $5 paint can lid. They also get the customer to come to the store for the paint and who knows what else they might buy when they are picking up the new can of paint to replace the dried out can of paint? They might buy more than a can of paint. What happens if the paint is thick but not yet dried out? Well, you touch up the wall with the thick paint and you wind up with a discolored wall. Now you must paint the entire wall. Which is most likely more than one can of paint, plus drop cloths, etc. All of which you might not have needed if you had bought a $5 paint can lid. So now you understand why the big box store has no interest in selling a $5 item that might cost them hundreds of dollars in sales.

You might think to yourself that you've got a product a customer would want to buy—but they can't buy something they've never heard of.

Sometimes you can't sell your product to big box stores because you only have one product. Today it is quite rare for buyers to buy a product from a new company that only has only one product. That's just the way it is. To get them to change their mind on your product, it would have to be incredibly special—and a sure winner—for them to take the chance. Too much work goes into dealing with a company that only has one product.

HOW DO YOU GET YOUR PRODUCT INTO THE LARGE CHAINS?

I can think of two ways.

1. You make a deal with a distributor that has a line of similar products selling into chain stores. You ride their relationship to success. Your team lawyer and broker will help you arrange a safe relationship with this distributor.

2. You sell your product yourself and build up a reputation and sales that cannot be ignored by the chains. If you're successful, the public will start asking for your product in the chain stores and the buyer of those stores will eventually seek you and your product out. To build that success you can sell your product on Amazon, YouTube, HSN, QVC, etc.

Sometimes you can't even sell you product on HSN or QVC, not because it's not a good product or one the public won't buy, but because you just can't sell it for enough money to entice HSN and QVC to give you the airtime. That is what happened to the inventor of the paint can lid went looking to be sold on TV.

If you believe in your product and you are prepared to spend not only the time but the money as well to market your product you have a chance to be successful. Never give up your dream until you have tried everything.

Sometimes a product doesn't sell because there's no real use for it. One person contacted me because they needed financing for, in his words, "the next billion-dollar product." He did have a solution for a problem people have. I even have the problem, so I was very interested in listening to his solution. The problem he was solving was stopping your plastic kitchen garbage bag from falling into the garbage pail when the bag got too heavy. We've all had that happen to us. He had the idea but had not done any real work on product development. The pictures this guy showed me were a couple of simple drawings of the metal cage he wanted to use to hold the garbage bag in place. He thought it would retail for $75-plus. Did I think he would make sales at $75? Yes. About four or five, maybe. There's always someone who will buy anything, but there are not always enough "someones" to make enough sales to drive your product to success.

This man's conceptions were crudely drawn by him and not by an engineer. The price was out of whack for what it did—and for a problem people might have six times a year. The inventor had no money to move forward. And, he had a bigger problem: me. I came up with a solution to the problem one minute after I said goodbye to him, and it cost only about 50 cents to solve.

CHAPTER 13

Are You an Inventor?

Many people look to start a business because they invented a new product or improved on one already in the market. Good for them. The world needs new inventions and product improvements.

THE DIFFERENT KINDS OF INVENTORS

I once belonged to an inventors' group. It was not because I had invented a product but because I felt I could help with the business aspect of getting a product to market and help with the financing. Half the group were inventors and half were people from different business backgrounds, such as marketing, law, and, like me, investment, and finance.

I must tell you, inventors are a strange bunch, and it was just so entertaining to be in a room with them. There are two kinds of inventors. The first is the most common: a person who invents a new product or improves an existing one. The second is a *businessperson* who invents a new product or improves on an existing one. The problem with inventors is that almost all are inventors but very few are businesspeople.

HERE'S WHAT I WITNESSED AT THESE MEETINGS:

Most of the people in the first group of inventors — the non-businesspeople—never got their invention to market. They trusted no one and were more concerned about someone stealing their idea than production and sales. They spent large amounts of money on the invention, even putting themselves into a terrible financial position—which in many cases prevented them from moving forward. And if by chance they did get their invention to market, most of the time it took too long and someone else had gotten something similar, but better, into the marketplace.

Most inventions should not require more than a year to go from idea, to prototype, to finished product but I would say the inventors in this group had been working on their inventions for an average of five years; two inventors I met had been at it for eight years, with no end in sight.

Although it is possible that someone will steal your idea it is highly unlikely to happen before it is brought to market. People do not steal what has not been proven to be successful. Why would anyone steal something with no proven market? People will steal the idea once they see you making money with it and that is why many people seek a patent for their invention. The patent, if granted, proves that the product in its design is yours, however, your patent is only as good as your pockets are deep. The legal fees to get a patent for inventions—many of which don't make it to market—are expensive and beyond that, it can be even more expensive to protect an invention. What most people don't understand about patents is that the government doesn't get involved with patent infringements. The government won't stop the product from coming into the country as long as the importing company pays the taxes and duties. If someone infringes on your patent it's up to you to stop them by suing the infringer. This is expensive. First, you'll need to find the person infringing on your patent, then you have to hire a lawyer to sue them in order to try and stop them.

Even if you successfully stop them and win a judgement in court, there is little-to-no-chance you will recover any money from the person infringing on your patent.

WHY DO PEOPLE INVENT THINGS?

There are a number of reasons why inventors invent things. Here are a handful:

- They had a problematic experience and came up with a solution
- They believe other people will benefit from their invention
- Once it gets out there, they will get a lot of recognition

- Once it catches on and people start buying it, they will make a lot of money

Most inventions never get off the ground because they don't work or don't serve any real beneficial purpose the public will pay for. Many of the inventions that work don't get off the ground because the inventor is not trusting, realistic, or a businessperson. The old saying that 50% of something is much better than 100% of nothing cannot be truer for these inventors.

Case in point: two inventors came up with a new device they wanted to take to market but they had exhausted their own finances and needed to find a partner to help them. Surprisingly, they found a company that was willing to provide the financing to produce the product, and to partner with them 50/50 and take it to market. What more could they want? Well, that was the problem. All they needed was some patience to reap the benefits of their new partnership, but they weren't patient. As a member of their inventors' group, they came to me in confusion because their new partner had just cancelled their partnership. I think I knew why the partnership was cancelled so I asked them a question to confirm my suspicion.

"Did you ask for money?" I asked

"Yes," came the answer.

"Why did you ask for money?" I asked.

"We have bills to pay," they said.

My response to them was "Go get a job."

Here were two guys who couldn't move their product forward—they had no money to do so—and they made the wise decision to partner up. And what did they do? They blew it because they were too lazy to get jobs. Other inventors would just run out of money and not make a deal that would provide them with the financing to continue because they could not accept giving away part of their invention to someone—through a partnership or by selling their idea for money and/or a royalty.

Meanwhile, a businessperson who invented a product would be happy they had found a deep-pocket partner who could take their product to market and would not ask them for help with the financing or have them guarantee the new financing. I met an inventor who came up with a way to produce wind power for homes without a windmill on the grounds. Granted, I'm not an engineer, but his concept of design, the thoroughness of the invention—from plan, design, costs, and manageability—were impressive. This seemed like an item that could be used in every house in every country, helping to reduce greenhouse gas emissions, improve air quality and fight climate change on a grand scale. They just had to scale the product down in size so it could sit on a roof. As it was presented to me, it took up the entire back of a pickup truck, so they were close to getting it to an appropriate size.

If this product worked, it would be a multi-billion-dollar idea that would be bought immediately for millions plus a royalty. The inventors had the ability to raise their own money from their homes through a new first or second mortgage, or they could look for a partner for the money they needed. However, they just wanted to get their money out instead of reinvesting their time and energy into a last push that would have brought us all into the millionaire stratosphere. That is where my business acumen sent me walking. I didn't need to be an engineer to know this invention would not work the way it was presented. These inventors either knew that and were just looking for someone to buy them out of their mistake, or they didn't have the vision to see what they were letting go of.

ISSUES AROUND PATENTS

Another person in the inventors' group had a product that had made it to market the previous year and it was quite successful for a first-year product. There were copies of his product coming into the country, however, even though the inventor had a patent on it. Imagine if that were you and the potential for this product to make you lots of money, based on its first-year performance projections, was pretty much guaranteed. Everything's looking great for you and your product, but now you find out that another company knocked it off and their copy is about to enter the country. How can this be? You have a patent for it and now their copies will be competing against your original. The government granted you a patent on this invention, so why isn't the government stopping product-copycats from coming into the country? The bottom line: it's not the government's job to police product-copycats from entering the country. The government's job is to protect its citizens and the environment from harm, not to protect the financial wellbeing of private companies from their competition.

So why would you even bother getting a patent from the government if they're not going to protect you? The government-issued patent protects you—i.e., your product—when you decide to fight against the copycats.

So, the member of the inventors' group with this successful first-year product asked for advice on what to do about the copycat item at one of our monthly inventors group meetings.

I asked him "do you have the money to pay a lawyer to protect the item?" He said, "I don't have it and I don't want to spend money I don't have fighting." I suggested he sell the rights to his product and the patent to the hardware chain that had had so much success with selling the item the year before. They'd have the pockets to protect the product from entering the market. They could pay him for his product either by buying the rights outright, paying him a royalty on every item sold, or a combination of both. I left the inventors group before finding out what the inventor did about the company that was bringing in a copy of his product. However, his product is still on the market all these years later and although I have looked for copycat products out of curiosity over the years, I have never found a similar product in any stores.

DO YOUR MARKET RESEARCH

A businessperson inventing a product will spend less time and money and will have better odds of succeeding when they do the research first. Here is my own example: my wooden fence's gate latch. After drilling holes for the sixth or seventh time, I got really fed up. If you're familiar with wooden fences, then you know that no matter how you fasten it, the latch rarely stays in place. I'm not an inventor or an engineer and I'm not even handy with tools. I believe in hiring professionals to fix your problems, so I wasn't about to start doing things myself. But I had an idea on how to fix the wooden gate latch problem that we all have.

Months prior to my most recent run-in with the latch on my fence, at one of the inventors' meetings, an engineering professor from one of the community colleges spoke about prototypes and what his students were doing at the time with 3D printers. I contacted him about developing a prototype for me. He said he would speak to his class and see if anyone had an interest in an outside assignment for bonus marks. One of his students was interested and we met. I selected a simple drawing from several designs I had come up with to show him what I wanted. He was interested in helping. He asked for $400 dollars, bought the materials, and made 10 samples for me. I really lucked out with this student.

Prototypes in hand, I set out to find a domestic manu-facturer. I chose domestic production even knowing it would cost me much more than going overseas. I wanted to be able to make changes easily, have some control over quality, buy smaller quantities, and be able to finance any large orders more easily. I found two manufacturers who were interested in taking on my project. Interestingly, neither one wanted the job if there was a possibility of large orders (more than 10,000 at a time).

We had used a die manufacturer out of Taiwan for the zinc die casting business so I decided to contact that company to see if they could help me. They had a satellite company in Seattle, Washington, which made it easier to deal with them than if had I had to deal directly with the factory in Taiwan. Their prices were 40-70% less expensive than other companies' prices, depending on quantity. I had them make a die for $2,000 (not expensive) and they sent me a dozen samples of each design and colour—which worked out to 48 pieces altogether—for the cost of shipping.

Then it was time for the packaging design. This is a two-step process. One is the artwork, and the other is the actual packaging. The artwork was easy, the packaging not so much. The product design and size made the packaging difficult. Neither shrink wrapping the item nor putting a plastic top (known as a clam shell) cover over the design made it look appealing. At the same time, I went to a large box company to discuss what boxes would work best for my product. What a lesson I got from the box company (you learn and gain experience everywhere)! First, most big box stores want products packaged six items to box. Apparently, they want small quantities because when they open a box, they want to put the entire box on the shelf and store the remaining full boxes in the warehouse. I had to figure out how many units would fill a pallet and determine whether I needed to box the small six-piece packages in a larger box or whether the retailer would accept an open pallet made up of six-piece boxes. The next item to discuss was the design of the box. Did the box manufacturer have a standard box that would work, or would I need to make my own die for the small box, and possibly the larger box, too?

It was tricky because I couldn't actually commit to a box design before getting an order since the big box store would probably have special requirements. I had previously sold fur earmuffs to Walt Disney World—yes, some of their visitors come from cold climates and who was I to argue?—and they had sent me three pages of instructions on how to package and deliver stock to their warehouse. So, I knew this was likely an important consideration. Which was beside the point because I had no orders yet; it wasn't time to worry about the boxes. But I did have to commit on the packaging. Which was also tricky because I knew it was quite possible that one or more of the box stores I hoped to sell to could want me to change the packaging.

I chose not to patent the idea because I knew it was easy to make changes to the design if someone wanted to copy it—so it wasn't worth patenting it. I would be the first into the market and that is generally good enough to secure an invention's position. I'd also be happy if someone wanted to buy my idea and pay me an ongoing royalty.

I came up with my idea in the summer and by the following May I was already exhibiting in Las Vegas at the largest hardware show in North America.

Getting your invention to market quickly is imperative. It will increase the likelihood of success and lessen the chances the product will be copied. My invention took less than a year to get in front of potential buyers because I was not scared to show my product to professionals who could move me along quickly. Most inventors don't get past their prototype within a year because they are more worried someone will steal their idea than focused on getting their idea to market.

Did the product work and solve a problem? Yes, better than anything else on the market. Did I make it a huge success? Financially, no. I never got the item moving mostly because I didn't give it the energy it needed. My business is financing sales to big box stores, not selling to big box stores and yet, I have no regrets because going through the exercise of getting an invention off the ground was priceless. What I learned producing the product will be rewarded by helping others move forward with their inventions.

Within 10 months and for under $20,000, I invented, designed, produced, packaged, and showed my product at the largest hardware show in North America. That might sound like a lot of money, and it is, but not compared to the time and money most inventors spend on getting their product in front of buyers.

CHAPTER 14

What Could Possibly Go Wrong?

Sometimes a financing deal is not exactly a cookie cutter situation, and one must think outside the box to get it completed. The account managers, aka the lenders' salespeople, rarely think outside the box to get a deal done. This is where an experienced broker can help turn a "no" into a "yes." An experienced broker is always better at presenting the financing opportunity to the lender than the business owner. An experienced broker will also know when to contact the person responsible for making the final credit decision if the deal *does* work but the lender's account manager does not see how it fits into the lender's structure.

STRUCTURING A DEAL

Since I know what the factoring companies are looking for, I can structure a deal that would be better for my client and still meet a factoring company's requirements. When businesses come to me for factoring, I don't just take the client to any factoring company, or the company with the best rates. I take them to the factoring company that specializes in their industry. I go to them looking for the kinds of arrangements I would provide a client. Many times, these are better terms than the factoring company might offer if the client were to call the factoring company directly.

One of the biggest worries a lender has about providing financing is how the business stands today—and will stand tomorrow—with the tax department. The tax department can and often does interfere with the assets of a business, even if those assets have been given as security to a lender. Like I said before, you never want to fight with the tax department, even if you're right and could win. They have the time and money to fight, and they don't always play fair. You might think you should have your lawyer or, even better, your accountant make arrangements with the tax department, but I've never met a lawyer—and I'm pretty sure I've never met an accountant—who actually knows how to deal with the tax department regarding arrears.

Taxes and Financing

Here is an example of a tax situation that will stop you in your tracks when looking for financing, regardless of what financing you are looking at.

A company found a factoring company that wanted to factor their $400,000 in invoices. They were behind with their tax remittance in the amount of $200,000 and the factoring company, during their due diligence, discovered the tax debt and were only *prepared to finance the invoices if they could use the first $200,000 to pay the tax arrears. This makes sense: the factoring company is getting a client and protecting themselves against the government garnishing receivables the factoring company has purchased. Now, if it were the other way around and the company owed $400,000 in taxes and only had $200,000 in receivables, it would be near impossible to get a factoring company to take them on until they had paid off their tax arrears.*

However, if that company used me as their broker, I would show the factoring company how they could purchase those receivables without any worry about the tax department garnishing the receivables. That is why you have a business broker as part of your team. Your team is there to be clever, visionary, smart and above all else to protect you and help you succeed beyond your dreams. Pick the right ones and you will never be alone. Don't think you need a team at the beginning? Then be prepared to spend a lot more of your time and money on everything that comes your way.

The old saying is so true when it comes to your team. "An ounce of prevention is worth a pound of cure."

HERE ARE SOME FORESEEABLE PROBLEMS YOU MIGHT FACE IN BUSINESS:

1. Growing too quickly for your current financing.

   Growing too quickly is a real problem and can possibly bankrupt your business. It's hard to believe, right? When you get an increase in business that you weren't expecting, you need to be able to afford to produce and deliver, otherwise your clients will find other suppliers. No business wants to turn down orders but if you take on business you cannot deliver on time, you risk losing that new client before delivering their first order.

   Even worse than disappointing a new client is when you disappoint an old one and you end up losing both the new client and the old one. To handle this increase in business, you need a plan on how you are going to pay for the increase in supplies, labor, equipment. Start by calling your accountant and broker and have a hard discussion on whether your business is operationally ready to take on new clients and expenses so quickly. Just because you can get the orders doesn't mean it's always good to take on every new order you get. If your business takes on these new expenses but fails to deliver the new orders, you have a big cash flow problem that your business might not survive.

   Sometimes you make more money saying, "no" to an order than saying, "yes."

2. Getting a contract that's too big for you to handle yet.

You don't want to lose the client before you ever do business with them. Sometimes you need to be honest (or very creative) when dealing with a new client order that's too large for your business to handle. So, how can you get the client to change their order without them knowing you are not able to deliver their order as presented to you?

The Dream and the Nightmare of Sudden, Unexpected Business Growth

A jeweler came to me looking for financing because a big box store wanted his product for 600 of their 2,000 stores. After he recovered from the shock of this unexpectedly large order, he was smart enough to start looking for money before committing to the order.

After thinking things through, he went to the big box store and suggested they test the product in their 200 best stores before rolling the program out to 600 stores. He got lucky and they agreed. That eliminated two thirds of the problem, but he still did not have the financing to deliver the order to the 200 remaining stores. The problem was not his ability to manufacture on time it was the fact he did not have the credit to get the gold for the entire order.

I came up with a great financing plan. The gold supplier would supply gold to the client's credit limit. The client would produce the order and bank the order in a secure place and give our company security on it. We would then pay off the gold supplier and the supplier would deliver the next round of gold. And the process would continue. This would happen three times before the entire order was completed and ready for shipment. Once the order was fully produced, it would be delivered, and we would buy the invoice (factor it) and pay off the purchase order financing we had done. We would give the manufacturer some of his profit and wait to get paid from the big box store.

The idea was so good that the gold supplier did the deal instead of us. Everything worked out for the supplier, the client, and the big box store but not so much for the people with the out-of-the-box idea.

3. Losing a very large client without a pipeline of new clients coming on board can cripple or even bankrupt your company.

    Earlier I mentioned a company in the zinc die casting business. They had everything going for them until their largest client got out of the business. Less than a year after going bankrupt the company began running a well equipment business that had gone from $100K to $300k-$400K a month; within18 months they were doing between $500-$600K a month. Things were humming: 50% of their debt to their new lender had been paid down (i.e., more than $500K had been paid down), they had money in the bank, and everything was running like a dream. I did warn the company's owners to look for new clients because it can take more than a year before you can start delivering large orders for a new client. They didn't listen and one day they got the call that their biggest client (about 40-50% each month of their sales) was getting out of the business.

Because I was involved, we made some drastic decisions quickly. We cut staff down to one shift, made new arrangements with our lender to slow down the paydown of the debt, and aggressively went after new business. The slower paydown really resulted in just a normalization of the repayment. This company had been paying off the debt so aggressively when everything was going well that they were more than two years ahead of schedule in retiring the debt. The lender was okay with the new repayment schedule. Lucky for the client.

It took more than a year to land a large new client, but the business did replace most of its lost business. Without the quick changes to the business and the help of the lender this business could have gone bankrupt. Your team is there to help.

4. A large client won't pay you or goes bankrupt.

Every B2B business will have a client who refuses to pay or who even goes bankrupt. There can be several reasons for payment refusals: the goods were not as ordered, they came late, the quality was not as expected, or they did not sell. None of these reasons should result in non-payment. A legitimate business would send goods back if they were not as ordered, or if quality was not as expected. Late delivery might be reason for a discount, but rarely for a return to the manufacturer (unless the goods are seasonal), and goods that don't sell are not the manufacturer's problem.

If you're not getting paid, demand the goods be returned to you immediately. At least this way you have your goods back. If the goods are returned, any that were sold should be paid for without a discount. If the goods are not returned and you don't get paid for the ones that sold, don't waste your time, go to your lawyer, and start a lawsuit. You can never allow the market to see that you can be taken advantage of.

You and your team need to sit down together and discuss how you are going to move forward, and what everyone's job will be in the move-forward plan. First, your broker will review your cash position and determine if there might be other financing arrangements available to you. The accountant will come up with a plan on how to deal with your suppliers, as you will have to ask for more time to pay. Your lawyer will handle any threats that come your way. You will call your bank if you have one and let them know what has happened. Let everyone who gives your business credit know what has happened and how you plan to move forward.

The only way to get out of this mess is to have a plan and have your creditors believe in the plan. By being proactive you are being responsible. You are also being the opposite of all the other debtors with whom creditors have problems. You have shown your creditors that you are not going to hide and that you have a plan and professionals to help with that plan.

When I first worked in the factoring business, we ran into a serious problem with one of our clients who, it seems, might have committed a little fraud. Lucky for me it was not *my* client. This is where I saw that being proactive with our creditors—in our case it was a private lender—and a bank was the right way to handle this problem.

By going to the private lender and the bank with a plan, the creditors did not panic and allowed us to resolve the problem without interference or a threat to our financing. The problem was resolved—more quickly than expected—and it built good will. Our lenders knew we were on top of the problem and had a plan to resolve it the best way possible. Our plan did not include getting every dollar back but, as it turned, out we did. We had under-promised and over-delivered.

5. Your business is growing, and a union wants in.

   This can be a nightmare for your business. Nothing good can happen for your business if a union gets in. I'm not saying unions are bad—unions stop companies from taking advantage of their employees. If you're good to your employees there's no reason for them to want to belong to a union. So, how do you keep the union out? Pretty simple. Ensure your employees are better off without the union than they would be with the union. Pay the same or a little more than the unions have negotiated and provide the same benefits—or better— than the union has arranged with other businesses. If the union gets in, you'll have to pay the higher wages and provide the benefits anyway. Why not make your employees happy, save the costs they'd have to pay through their union dues, and save your company the headache of having to deal with a union? Implement automatic increases to pay and benefits to match what unions can achieve in businesses in which they are represented.

Even if you pay the same—and you can't pay less—and provide the same benefits as unionized businesses there is no reason for you employees to want a union. They are financially ahead without the union because they're not paying union dues and can't be forced out on strike.

The only employees who will still want a union are the lazy ones who want to take advantage of the union protecting them when they don't do their job to your satisfaction. These are not employees you want working for you anyway, so give them notice and be done with them. Union or no union, you want your workers to be happy. Happy workers show up on time, care about their work, and work better because they have a well-paying job. And they keep their job by doing their job properly. Unions cause interruptions with strikes, walkouts, and other threats. None of those things happen in non-union businesses.

Not All Union Demands Are Created Equal

Many years ago, a tire manufacturer had a union in place. The union went to management to demand pay increases. The company said, "we can't afford any raises or increases to benefits or pensions if we are to stay in business." The union didn't believe them, demanded the increases, and threatened to go on strike. The company opened their books to the union's accountants to prove they were unable to meet the union's demands. The union's accountants reported it was true, the company was not able to meet any of the union's demands (these were the union's own accountants) and the union should back down for now.

Nonetheless, the union maintained their demands, and when those demands were not met, they went on strike for four weeks. Eventually the company gave in to their demands. You can imagine after four weeks without pay how happy the employees were to be going back to work with their higher wages and better benefits. Only one problem: when the employees showed up to work after the strike was over, they found the gate locked and a sign letting them know that the company was permanently closed and had relocated to the US. The union was successful in getting their demands met but the business closed because the union was more concerned with winning concessions than making sure their unionized workers had jobs.

* * * * *

About Strikes

Have you ever noticed that strikes will last either a couple of days or go on for weeks and even months before a company gives in to the workers' demands?

The reason for this: math. For every week an employee is away from work on the picket line, they must receive a 2% increase in the first year to make up for the lost pay. So, when a worker is out for four weeks, they must receive an 8% increase in the next 12 months to make up for the income they lost over the four weeks they were on strike. If they only get a 4% raise it will take them two full years to break even for the four weeks of lost pay.

1. Your client wants a big discount because the order is late and will not accept it otherwise.

   How much are they asking for? Why, is the order late? Most times a request for a discount is about 10%—but what do you do when the customer wants more? Bear in mind that the 10% is not really 10%. Here is why: if you charge $10 for each unit you sell, and they cost $7 per unit to produce, then the 10% discount of $1 is 33% of your $3 profit.

   First, let's discuss the client. Is this a very important client? Has the order ever been late before? How late is the order? Why was it late? Who else can deliver the same order to them in the future?

   If this is a large, older, and loyal client, then it would be in your best interest to give them the 10% discount and apologize. If the order was late because it was your company's fault, then eat the discount, keep your client happy, and make sure it does not happen again. If the order is only one or two days late and this is a new client, maybe this is not a company you want to do business with. I wouldn't give them the discount. In fact, I would suggest that if they're not willing to accept the order without the discount, then they should return the entire order. I'm pretty sure you'll be better off taking the goods back and selling them to someone else than hoping you'll get paid anywhere close to on time. If they make this demand over an order that was only a couple of days late, I guarantee it won't be the only headache this client will give you.

If they want more than a 10% discount, I suggest refusing any discount, keep the order and sell it to other clients over time. If it takes you a year to sell the entire order, you'll be further ahead financially than if you had given them a discount larger than 10%.

If the client ever says to you that if they do not get the discount they will take their business elsewhere, I can guarantee you that nine out 10 times they're going to take their business elsewhere even if you give them the discount. Worry about this order and not promises of future business. It's better to make money on this order and not do business with this client again than to give them the discount and hope they give you more business in the future.

2. A major supplier doesn't deliver on time and jeopardizes your client's order.

This is going to happen, so you need a back-up plan. Call this your supplier insurance. You should know every supplier that can deliver this product. You want to know how fast they can deliver, their costs, quantities, and lead time. I would even suggest you buy from some or all the other suppliers from time to time, just so they know who you are, and this will make them more willing to deliver larger quantities when you are in a pinch.

They will do this if only for their own selfish reasons, i.e., hoping to get a large percentage of your business.

When you have a large order to get out to a good client, you need to do whatever is necessary to deliver that order and keep your client happy. Sometimes that means taking a hit on your profit because you need to use a more expensive supplier when your regular supplier lets you down.

So, what should you do if this happens? First, call up your supplier and see if they can arrange for another supplier to deliver your order. If they can, they will generally eat any increase in the price. They are going to do what you are prepared to do: get the order out to keep their client (you) happy.

If there is going to be a delay delivering the order, call your client to let them know what is happening. They're going to find out anyways, so it's better to be pro-active about it. You may find your client is unable to accommodate the late order and then there is no need to find higher-priced suppliers. If they're unable to accommodate the late order, your willingness to meet your commitment by finding alternative production sources will go a long way to ensuring your client views you as a supplier they can count on.

Sometimes your clients will insist you carry inventory they can draw on quickly. If this is the case, problem solved. Before agreeing to this, though, know what you're getting your business into with your limited cash flow tied up in inventory. This is something your team will help you with.

Inventory Issues

I knew a bottle cap supplier that had some clients who required them to keep a certain amount of inventory on hand for every contract, even if delivery wasn't scheduled for a year later. This was both risky and expensive for the manufacturer. What if the client cancelled the order—as was their right? What would the manufacturer do with the extra "specialized" inventory they had on hand? So, an agreement was struck that if the client cancelled the order before the end of the contract—or even at the end of the contract—they still had to pay for the excess inventory they required. The manufacturer was protected against being stuck with inventory for a cancelled contract and the client always knew there was inventory available.

3. Difficulty finding staff.

   Unless you intend to remain a one-person operation, you'll eventually need to hire employees.

When it comes to hiring, there's no bigger waste of time and money than hiring the wrong employee.

Hiring Hourly Employees

If these are your first employees, then you're probably stuck with doing the interviewing and hiring. If you're lucky, you know someone who's done this before and will help you. Ask them to do it and let them do it. You still need to meet the candidates and make the final decision, but you don't have to do the interviewing.

Most mistakes involving the hiring of hourly workers, are easy to correct by just letting them go. Most mistakes that will give you reason to let an employee go will occur within the three-month probation period. If you let them go during the probation period, you don't owe severance pay. Make it clear to everyone you hire that they are on a three-month probation.

If you already have management in place overseeing your hourly workers, let them do the hiring and firing. Try your best to stay out of this unless management calls you in.

Hiring Management Positions

Meet all the candidates yourself. Give them an idea of what you are looking for from them and let them know that someone else will be doing the interviewing for the candidates that you select to move on in the hiring process. Have someone else do the interviewing if you can. You can use a permanent placement agency: although costly, it is generally effective. Use only companies that charge a fee that includes several, if not unlimited, hirings for that specific position. What I mean is that the agency will continue to find suitable candidates for that position if the person they put forward and whom you hire does not work out within a certain timeframe. Their fee comes with a guarantee you will be happy with the person they recommend you hire, or they will find another person at no cost until you are happy.

The agency is going to ask a lot of questions that you will not, either because you do not know to ask them, or you are uncomfortable asking certain questions.

Remember I did the interviewing and hiring of my first secretary? She fit all the criteria I was looking for and a week later I had to let her go from a job any preteen could have handled. After that, I never did any of the interviewing when hiring a secretary, I always had other people handle it for me with better success. In one situation I used a permanent placement agency to hire a new secretary for me. After a long list of candidates were interviewed, the agency came to me with two suitable candidates and different reasons to consider each one. The first one was a younger woman a job or two out of school. The second one was about 10 years older. Both were more than qualified for the job.

So, let's discuss the concerns the agency had for both. The first one had a job record from before, during and after school that showed her longest term at a job was about one year—the year after she had finished school. The second candidate concerned them because she'd be taking a pay cut of almost $10,000 and they were worried she would stay only until she could find a higher-paying job. And there was another concern: all her past employers were unionized. Through their interviewing they determined this could be a problem if she were asked to do something that might take her past the end of the day or was not part of her original job description. She was comfortable knowing there would be parts of the day with not much to do. She wasn't keen on staying a little late or maybe having to come in on a Saturday at year end. Had I conducted the interviews myself I never would have thought to ask the kinds of questions the agency had asked.

The only job where I have done my own hiring is when I've been looking for salespeople and no one other than me would know who the right person might be.

4. A large client is demanding lower prices and threatening to go to your competitor.

    This is a scary and complicated situation. Do you lower the prices or let the client go?

    The first question to ask yourself is this: "How much of a discount are they demanding and what percentage of my profits will I be giving up?" Keep in mind that a 10% discount could mean 20%-100% of your profits, depending on the kind of business you are in and the mark-ups you take.

    If you can't afford to meet the discount, let them go. You're in business to make money, not spin your wheels. This lower price demand isn't just to get a lower price so they can make more money. Chances are high they were either approached by one of your competitors with a lower price to win their business, or they're getting squeezed by their own clients for better pricing and they're coming to you to make up that profit loss for them.

The second question to ask yourself is this: "Is there a competitor to take this business to, and do I think this competitor will give the client the price they want?" If you think your competitor can and will give them the better price, you have a problem.

If you can't afford the lower price, then most likely your competitor can't either, or they are prepared to cut corners to give the lower price. Let them do it. You know how much your product costs to produce. Unless your competition has come up with a new cost-saving way to produce the items you do not know about, they are cutting corners or spinning their wheels just to get the business. Businesses that take on unprofitable orders just for cash flow are doomed to fail. Never take on business that is not going to give you sufficient profit.

And the third question to ask yourself is this: "What percentage of my overall business does this client represent?" If the client makes up 10% or less of your business, stand your ground and say, "no" to lowering your prices. However, if your client makes up more than 10% of your revenue, there's more to consider before giving or refusing the discount your client demands. Review what investments you've made in order to service this client. Did you invest in special or extra equipment? Have you taken on extra employees to handle this client's business? If you have bank financing, how will this affect it?

And always ask this question about any demanding client: "What will their next big ask be?"

When a client demands discounts or unacceptable terms and threatens to take their business elsewhere if you do not agree, it's time to sit down with your accountant and broker before you make any decisions.

You and your team will assess the direct overhead related to this client including equipment, employees, commodity contracts, rental space, and any other directly related costs. If any or all of the above are being used only for that client, you need to look to relieve your business of these expenses. Sell the equipment, let the extra employees go, see if you can stretch the commodity contracts out over a long period of time, or see if you can sell part of your contract. The only thing you can do about excess rental space is to try and sublet it. The savings from cutting these expenses will probably cover a large percentage of the profits you will be losing from letting this client go.

5. Your client is now demanding longer payment terms from you.

   There is no good news to be found when a client is demanding longer payment terms from you.

   In essence, the client is looking for your business to finance their business. They want their clients to pay them before they pay you. You're not in the financing business unless you're a lender and let them know that. If they threaten to move to another supplier, let them go immediately. They have just let you know they are in financial trouble.

With today's interest rates being so low, it is more profitable for your client to pay you in 10 days less a 2% discount than it is for them to take 90 days to pay you. The 2% discount is higher than the interest rates their bank is charging them for 90 days of financing. This is also a great way to test the financial wellbeing of your client. When you present them with the 2% 10-day discount, they should either keep the terms you have with them or take the 2% 10-day discount. If they stand firm on their demand for 90 days, they have financial problems, and you should consider tightening your terms with them not extending them.

6. Your supplier drastically raises their prices or the commodity you buy is going up quickly.

    This is every business's nightmare. Your supplier gives you no notice that their prices were going up and there's no way for you to raise your prices on a firm order from your client.

    So, what do you do? You bite the bullet for this order and let your client know your supplier raised their prices, and you will have to raise yours on future orders. Then you hope your client is okay with the increase. This is exactly why you add 10% to your costs, for the miscellaneous, "who knows what." You're welcome!

When your business uses a commodity such as zinc, copper, nickel etc.—and it's a major component in your production—you must take steps to protect against rapid increases in that commodity and this should always be included in every sales contract. The first way to stabilize your prices is to add a protection clause to your sales contracts with your clients. It should state there will be an automatic increase or decrease in prices based on the price of the commodity that goes into your product. So, if the commodity takes a big jump up or down you can adjust your price accordingly without the worry that your client will cancel the contract. The trigger could be 5%-10% increase or decrease in the price of the commodity at the start of the contract. Remember, this works both ways. You must decrease your price if the price goes down from the agreed amount just as you will increase it if the price goes up.

Another way to stabilize your prices is to buy futures contracts in the commodity you use. This gives you a fixed cost of the commodity that you use over a certain period. It also does not affect any conditions you have in the contract around changing the price. In other words, if the price of the commodity goes up you get to increase your prices by the amount you and your client agreed to in your contract, even if the price you are paying doesn't go up because you have a futures contract. Again, it works both ways, so it is best not to lock your business into a commodity contract that forces you to buy all of the commodity at the contract price during the contract term. Make sure your contract allows you to buy the commodity at the spot price (that day's price) when the price dips.

Commodity Contracts Can Lead to Great Savings

In the zinc die casting business mentioned earlier in the book, we entered into a zinc contract to purchase 2,500,000 pounds of zinc at a fixed price. At the time, this represented about 65% of the zinc we would use in a year. We didn't have to take a specific amount of zinc every month, but we did need to draw it all down within a year or 18 months. This allowed us to take advantage of the low zinc spot prices at the time and keep our contract pricing available to us as prices increased.

When prices increased, we started to draw down on our low-priced contract, and we were not obliged to pass the savings onto our clients. Since zinc prices hit the price we had agreed would trigger a raise in the cost to the customer, we were able to raise our prices even though the price we were paying for zinc was much less than the spot price of zinc. I believe the contract earned us about $20,000 a month in savings, which went straight to our bottom line.

These commodity contracts are a way to protect against wild fluctuations in commodity prices but remember that sometimes prices go down and you must pay the higher price laid out in your contract.

It's best to make sure you have as long as possible to draw down on the contract.

There are two wins and one loss on a commodity contract. The two wins are a lower locked-in price and a fixed cost you can count on for the term of the contract. The one downside is that if the commodity really takes a nosedive, then you could be stuck paying a higher price as you draw down (as slowly as possible) on the contract. Again, this is where the 10% for "the who knows what" really comes in.

7. Unforeseen problems that are no fault of your own such as Covid-19.

    Things happen that are not your fault, yet they still affect your business. It could be a storm, a fire in the building where your business is housed, or a global pandemic. These are good reasons to keep your team up to speed with your business. This way, when the unexpected happens, your team is ready to help immediately. If you don't have your team in place already, you will find yourself scrambling to find a new lawyer, accountant, and/or a business broker. And you will lose valuable time, and possibly a lot of money, getting them up to speed.

    Let's imagine a storm destroys your factory. Your business is closed, your revenue is zero. You still have expenses, and your creditors are not interested in waiting. Of course, the first call you make is to the insurance company and of course, the insurance company is going to do everything possible to give you as little as possible. If the insurance company senses any desperation on your part, you'll get less over a longer period.

Your team is incredibly important in a situation like this. Your lawyer makes sure you are not only protected but—and this is the most important thing—that the insurance company knows you have the money and the staying power to fight them. Your accountant helps your lawyer by proving to the insurance company the size of the losses your business incurred because of the storm that destroyed your factory and business. And your broker plays a big part as you move forward with contracts, financing, and dealing with your creditors.

It's impossible to be prepared to handle every challenge that might arise in the course of running your business but if you use your common sense—and have a good team around you—you'll be able to get through the many ups and downs that go with the territory.

CHAPTER 15

What Else Could Go Wrong ...and Right?

I had a client in textiles whose business was ruined by a fire. Without his lawyer and me, his broker, the damage would have shut his business down. This client sold textiles to large chains, and he also produced items under contract to other textile/sales companies. Each one of those clients brought in an insurance company to assess the losses.

How did the fire start? Well, at the end of the workday a seamstress forgot to shut off her machine and that night an electrical storm caused a power surge resulting in a very small, and contained, fire. Meanwhile, the fire caused the sprinklers to go off and the alarm went off, too, bringing in the fire department. By the time the sprinklers were turned off and the fire department finished putting out this small fire, the entire factory was flooded and everything in the factory was ruined. One little fire. Had someone been there, it would have been put out with a fire extinguisher. Instead, it destroyed a factory and almost ended a business. This happened during the pandemic and caught everyone off guard.

Which brings us to another point: even the companies that greatly benefitted from the pandemic weren't ready for what came their way. Businesses such as delivery companies, producers of disinfection products, large box stores (when small stores couldn't open) etc., all eventually came away with stronger and more profitable businesses because of the pandemic. But businesses that could not open—or could not fully open because the governments wouldn't let them—had to fight to survive. The government did their best to help but some of these businesses lost everything...because they were not prepared for when S**t happens.

Here's another example –

BUSINESS V. THE PANDEMIC

The government forced a franchise tutoring business to close temporarily, and the owner decided she didn't want to re-open even when the government allowed her to reopen. She had two problems: the first is that she was part of a franchise, and the second was that she had personally guaranteed a lease with a large landlord.

She had bought the franchise from another franchise owner and signed the lease without a lawyer reviewing it first. Even though the government closed her business the franchisor and the landlord did not want to let her out of their monthly franchise fees and rent payments. Instead of seeking the help of a lawyer, the owner spoke to a friend who suggested she go to a trustee in bankruptcy and bankrupt her business. She sought the advice of a trustee who was only too happy to bankrupt her business for a flat fee of $15,000. Lucky for her, that same friend is a friend of mine and just happened to mention her situation to me.

I suggested she call me before signing up with the trustee. We spoke for about an hour, and I found out that the franchisor did not have a personal guarantee from her and could only go after her business for any monies owing. Now, as far as her landlord was concerned, she had more than two years left on her lease with about $77,000 in total rent still owing, and she had personally guaranteed the rent. To make matters worse, there was equity available in a condominium she owned and because she had given the landlord a personal guarantee the landlord could go after the equity in her condominium if her business did not pay the remaining rent.

If she had used the trustee, she would have paid the trustee $15,000 to bankrupt her company which would have done nothing to solve the $77,000 in rent she personally owed because she owned her condominium and had given a personal guarantee to the landlord. And no, personal bankruptcy was not an option. The equity in the condominium prevented her from going personally bankrupt to get out of paying the outstanding rent.

While the government had closed the business, the franchisor claimed my client owed $3,200 in back payments plus $10,000 for what I still do not understand, plus future franchise fees. The company owned nothing other than some furniture and some marketing materials. Since they did not have a personal guarantee from the franchisee and the business had no other assets for them to claim, we made a settlement for a one-time final payment of $1,600. Franchisor problem ended. By the way, for $15,000, the Trustee could have saved the $1,600 she paid in a settlement to the franchisor.

Now it was time to deal with the real problem: the landlord holding her personal guarantee. I asked for a copy of the lease and reviewed it with my lawyer. This is where a lawyer is so valuable. Turns out there was a clause in the lease to protect the landlord should something "that was no fault of their own" happen which prevented the landlord from giving the rental unit to the tenant when they were supposed to. This might include a delay in the construction completion date, a fire, or a flood, etc. Well, what's good for the landlord is good for the tenant. The clause allowed the tenant to stop rent payments while she was closed by the government and, even better, she would not owe any of the back rent when she was allowed to re-open. Basically, the rent was forgiven. **NOTE**: This clause is not in every lease agreement, so have your lawyer review your lease to find out if it's in yours or not.

Obviously, the landlord did not agree with our interpretation of the clause, but the tenant was holding firm and made it clear she was willing to fight over this clause. She offered $10,000 as a settlement against all remaining lease payments. About a month later, the landlord and the tenant agreed on a $15,000 settlement.

This was a great win for the tenant, however had she gone to a lawyer when she bought the franchise, she likely would not have signed a personal guarantee. This would have saved her the $15,000 she ended up giving to the landlord, my fee, and all the stress this situation caused.

PERSONAL RESPONSIBILITY FOR LEASES

I was also referred to a massage therapist who had been in business for less than one year and wanted out of her lease when the government closed her down because of the pandemic. I was happy to find her lease was written up on a real estate offer-to-lease form—an easy one to get out of. That is, until I found out she was a sole proprietor and therefore everything was essentially in her personal name and guaranteed personally. When I asked why she wasn't incorporated she said her accountant didn't feel it was necessary as she was just opening.

Well, too bad she listened to her accountant. Had she been incorporated, she could have just removed her equipment and walked away with no push back on her personally. That wasn't the case so there was nothing I could help her with other than to suggest she try to make a new deal with the landlord when she was allowed to open again.

HERE'S ANOTHER SITUATION YOU MIGHT FIND YOURSELF IN...

Creative Financing: A Hypothetical Situation

A business with little credit history finds themselves needing a large piece of equipment for a very profitable job they have won. The owner finds the piece of equipment needed for $150,000, however the manufacturer does not provide credit terms and directs the owner to a leasing company that handles all their lease inquiries. The leasing company does their due diligence and turns down the lease request. Why? In all cases the turndown is based on the creditworthiness of the business looking for the lease financing. Either the company's credit is not very good, or the company is too new to have established a credit history.

You might be asking yourself why the leasing company would turn down the lease when the company has been awarded a very profitable job. The leasing company does not take into consideration the new contract that the business has been awarded. The reason is that the leasing company does not know if the company can deliver on the order even with the new equipment in place. If they cannot deliver on the order, they will not have the funds to make their lease payments.

The owner decides to take out a second private mortgage on his or her home to fund the purchase. The owner engages a mortgage broker to secure a mortgage large enough to buy the piece of equipment. After the broker completes the due diligence process, the broker informs the owner that there is only $50,000 available from a second mortgage. Generally, this would be the end of the discussion. The owner does not buy the piece of equipment and must turn down the contract. The manufacturer loses out on a $150,000 sale. The leasing company loses out on providing a lease. And the mortgage broker does not earn a commission on the mortgage.

A business broker who thinks out of the box presents a solution that might provide the necessary financing. With the $50,000 available from the second mortgage, the business broker approaches the leasing company with a proposal, saying, "The owner is prepared to take out a $50,000 second mortgage and use the funds as a down payment for the piece of equipment. Would you be willing to provide a $100,000 lease to the businessowner?" This is an entirely new lease concept: instead of a 100% lease, this is only a 65% lease. The business is willing to put real skin in the game and is prepared to risk his/her home to make this deal work. The equipment is easy to resell, especially when they only have 65% into the deal.

Outcome: The leasing company does the deal. The owner is happy and can take on the big contract, the leasing company is happy because they just did a 65% loan-to-value lease deal, the mortgage broker is happy and earned a commission on the mortgage, the manufacturer is happy they sold a $150,000 piece of equipment and the business broker is happy to help his client and make a fee on the lease. Everyone wins. Why? Because the business broker had the experience, talent, vision, and creativity to think outside the box.

Bad things happen all the time to good hardworking people, but it doesn't mean you can't make it. Think things through and make a plan—even if it means closing and reopening when things get back to normal. Many people did everything they could during the pandemic—and at other times throughout history— to keep going. Except for one thing: close and wait for better times. Business owners borrowed money, held back their tax remittances, and cut prices, just to keep going. All this put the business and business owner further in debt and financially jeopardized their personal and business lives.

And When Your Team is in Place...

Any business with a team in place before the pandemic was in a much better position to survive the economic downturn and maybe even prosper because of the opportunities the pandemic provided. Their team would have helped determine if closing or changing course might put the owner in a position to take advantage of new ways of doing business, starting a new business, or buying a business at a very favorable price. If someone incurred debt by staying open and their creditors start calling for their money, the first and most important thing is to not ignore them. If they call, answer the phone, or call them back. If they email you, email them back immediately. You need to show you are not running away from your responsibilities.

Then, with all the information on the debts you owe, you can go to your team and start working on a repayment plan. Obviously, your creditors want to get paid immediately. That's not possible and will not be part of the plan. Once your creditors know you are not even entertaining paying them off immediately but that you have full intentions of honoring your obligations you can start putting your plan in place.

Your creditors will work with you if they see reasonable efforts on your part and that you have a plan in place that makes sense. Remember: they need you to stay in business if they want to get paid. They have lost enough money and clients to bankruptcy already; they cannot afford to lose you as well. Therefore, both you and your creditors need to work together for you to stay in business, and for them to get paid and keep you as an ongoing client.

Asking your accountant to put a financial plan together for paying your debts and keeping the business going shows you are serious about moving forward successfully and that there is a reasonable plan to do so.

Your lawyer will handle any demands or threats creditors make. Creditors who are not willing to work with you are going to have a very difficult time collecting when they are fighting with your lawyer rather than with you. Just having a lawyer will bring creditors to the table who might not have been willing to talk if you were defending yourself. Plus, businesses do not spend money on professionals if they're not planning to stay in business and pay their creditors, so this sends a signal to your creditors that you are serious about getting financially back on track.

Your business broker is very important—at times even more important than your lawyer or accountant. Your broker directly negotiates with creditors. He or she needs to be good enough and tough enough to make sure creditors understand what happens if they accept or do not accept your go-forward plan. This plan is going to call on your creditors to be patient with the repayment of the debt, as well as continuing to provide you with ongoing products or services for your business. Any creditors who are not willing to support your plan to continue your business will have to sue your business and hope you stay in business to pay them years down the road.

One of your creditors is most likely the tax department for tax arrears. Your broker should know how to deal with the tax department for your plan to work. Unless the tax department buys into your plan, you will have little to no chance of succeeding. If your broker knows what he or she is doing, they will not let the tax department bully you into a repayment schedule you can't afford. A good broker will be able to arrange with the tax department what your business can afford while also using the tax department to get your creditors onside with your plan. Your creditors are in jeopardy of not getting paid if the tax department doesn't work with you, so your broker can use that in the repayment negotiations with your creditors.

What you and your team are doing is providing a professional, well-thought-out solution to your creditors, which is a plan they are unlikely getting from any of their other debtors. This makes you look like a business they want to work with, not fight with.

Summary Thoughts

Whether you're in the start-up phase of a new business or buying an existing business you will find there are many unknowns and much you can't predict until it happens. All your excitement, belief, plans, and vision will help lead you to sales and growth but if you rely only on yourself none of it will get you out of trouble in a timely and creative fashion. To mitigate problems as they arise, every business needs to start with…

A Business Plan

Go through the exercise of writing the plan. Whether what goes in there actually happens in the way, timing, and order that your plan lays out doesn't matter. The exercise is a teaching one and all new business owners should start with a plan.

You Need a Marketing Plan

In the movie *Field of Dreams*, the father of the character played by Kevin Costner used to tell him, "If you build it, they will come." Well, don't believe it. No one's running to buy from you. Set something in place. Decide where and how you want to market to your potential new clients and do this consistently in your start-up phase. Even a small budget is better than none.

Downsized Your Personal Financial Life

When you start a business, pay everyone else before you pay yourself because if your business can't pay its bills it will cease to exist. You're the last person to get paid so that basically means in the first two years or so, your personal needs come after those of your business.

Make Sure You Have Some Money in the Bank

You—and if you have a family, your family, too—will have to survive on less for at least six months, probably longer. If you have a spouse or are very young and are lucky to have parents who can contribute to personal expenses, it'll take a great deal of stress and financial pressure off your back until the business builds momentum.

Create a Solid Sales Strategy

Like it or not, once you start a business, you're in sales. A company that isn't making sales isn't going to be around for very long so you're going to have to figure out how to close deals. Work on sales scripts, contracts, proposals, and whatever else will get interested buyers to say, "yes."

You're Going to Need Some Stamina

Kiss the 9-to-5 goodbye. You will work harder than you've ever worked to make your business succeed. You need to be prepared to work 10–18-hour days sometimes seven days a week.

And no serious-minded person would be wise to start a new business without a team of professional advisors on hand.

OTHER ADVICE I CAN OFFER?

Sometimes you make more money saying "No" to an order than you do saying, "yes."
The promise of future business should never be considered when you are asked to do something that is not a benefit to your business. Never lower your prices on the promise of future business, never compromise your integrity on the promise of future business, and never give concessions to companies on the promise of future business. The future business either never comes or you are not put in a position to make money on it.

You're in business to make money, so be smart about it and make money!
How much your clients are willing to pay for your products is none of your business. Sell your products for the amount you need to earn to make it worthwhile to be in business. If no one wants to pay your price for what you sell, find a new business. Do not lower your price to meet your clients' price demands. If you do, the question won't be IF you'll go out of business, the question will be WHEN you will go out of business.

The relationship you have with your professional team of advisors is more than a business arrangement; it's a partnership. Don't settle when it comes to choosing each member of this team. They have eyes, ears, contacts, and skillsets that you don't have, unless you yourself are in legal, financial, or negotiations-related fields. You want an accountant and lawyer who will treat you like you are their biggest and most important client. Always pay them on time to ensure your calls are taken. You want a broker who understand business from every angle and perspective. One who listens but isn't afraid to be honest with you about the realities of the sale and negotiation process.

If you've read this far, I'm guessing you are determined to start your new business and do everything you possibly can to make it succeed. I hope this book has given you some ideas about what to watch out for when you start your own business, and I hope you've found some value in the information I've shared. I might not know you, but I'll be wishing you well on your business journey and hoping you're able to move forward with as few problems as possible. There will be problems. But for just about every problem there is also a solution and it's my wish that you will be able to find your way to those solutions so your business can thrive and so your family can prosper. In case I haven't been clear (which I kind of doubt, at this point), a great team is the cornerstone of that plan for the future.

Let me know if I can help.
Michael Yasny
January 2022
michael@moneyconsultants.ca
www.moneyconsultants.ca

Appendix

EXAMPLES OF OUTSIDE-THE-BOX FACTORING IDEAS

Long term factoring deals: Most factoring companies will not buy an invoice that has payment terms longer than 90 days. Some won't buy them if they have terms of more than 60 days. This is because of the cost—it's too expensive for the client—and it's also too hard to margin the invoice at their bank. Banks, like factoring companies, don't want to be financing invoices over 90 days—some won't go over 60 days. Here are some ideas of what we've done before to help people keep their business going during challenging times.

Deal #1: An office goods supply company.

This was a good business, but it did not have the $500,000 cash or credit it needed to take advantage of a government relocation opportunity. The government was prepared to give the company $500,000 to move one of its offices but the company had to put up $500,000 to get the government money. I was approached by the owners to see how I could help them with the $500,000. The client had been selling long-distance services to their office supply clients and had earned over $2,000,000 in commissions, with $1.4 million due in the next 12 months; the remainder was to be paid within about 18 months.

I took the deal to the financial officer and the owner of the factoring company. This was a big deal so they did their due diligence but came back with a "no" because they couldn't finance it with their bank due to its margining requirements which dictated they could only finance invoices that were less than 60 days old. I asked them if they thought the long-distance reseller was creditworthy and if they would buy 60-day receivables from them. The answer was, "yes" and "yes." I asked if they believed the $2,000,000 was real. They answered "yes." Then I asked, "If the bank said you could margin the receivable for 12 months would you buy the receivable?""Yes" again.

My out-of-the-box suggestion was this: Let's take assignment of the entire $2,000,000 in commission due. Let's create a $600,000 invoice. Each month there will be a commission payment due that we will put towards the $600,000 invoice. At the end of 60 days, we will refactor the remaining amount of the $600,000 invoice and treat it as a brand-new invoice. This solves your margining problems, provides the client with the $500,000 they need to get the government to give them $500,000, and we get to factor a $600,000 invoice.

We bought the deal, and everyone was happy.

Deal #2: A company that produced equipment for Sirius XM Radio.

The equipment was valued at about $30,000,000 and came with a warranty. The warranty was expiring, and Sirius XM wished to pay for a warranty extension. The price for the extended warranty was $130,000 per month, which Sirius XM was willing to pay. The client wanted to sell an entire year's warranty to the factoring company. The factoring company was concerned that if the company closed there would be no one to service the warranty. This was a legitimate concern. The only solution was to find another company capable of completing the warranty if necessary, at which point the factoring company would advance against the contract. The factoring company was also willing to advance only 60% of the gross contract, as opposed to their usual 80% advance rate on invoices. The owners felt they needed a buffer in case they had to pay another company to do the work and, what's more, the fees on this deal would have eaten most of the 20% reserve they typically held back.

The deal didn't go through because the client wasn't prepared to take only a 60% advance and would only move forward if they were advanced 75%. The factoring company chose to walk away. Turns out there was a problem with the company, and it was a good thing the factoring company walked away. Sometimes you do better to just say no on a deal.

Deal #3: A company that made corrugated pallets.

At times this company had to purchase wooden pallets to supply to their clients. They found a wooden pallet supplier, but the supplier would not give the client credit. So, the client approached me for purchase order financing, or what my company called a supplier guarantee. It's principally the same thing. I approached the wooden pallet company with a financing option: they would give my company credit and I would pay them in 30 days. They did a credit check on my company and agreed to a credit limit that met everyone's needs. But I added a very special condition to the financing: every single order had to be okayed by me in writing through a supplier guarantee. Simply put, the wooden pallet manufacturer would forward the purchase order from the corrugated pallet company to me and if I agreed to the purchase, I'd provide the pallet company with a signed supplier guarantee. The supplier guarantee was my company's guarantee to the wooden pallet manufacturer that they would be paid in 30 days.

If the wooden pallet manufacturer did not have my written supplier guarantee, then I was not guaranteeing payment on the purchase order, and they shouldn't expect payment from my company if they did deliver.

Everything worked out well for about six months. Then for some reason the wooden pallet company started shipping pallets to the corrugated pallet company without the supplier guarantees attached. Since there were no purchase orders or invoices for me to rely on or factor, and I had not issued the supplier guarantee, I didn't pay those invoices. The wooden pallet company came looking for payment and I said, "No. We had an agreement that I would only pay you on purchase orders where I had issued a supplier guarantee." I asked if they had been paid on time for every single supplier guarantee, and they answered "yes." So, we had an agreement, I had lived up to my end of it, they didn't, and they had shipped without the signed supplier guarantee. Why should I pay them?

Even though we had done about $200,000 in business over six months without a problem, the wooden pallet company lost about $80,000 on invoices they should never have lost a penny on because they got lazy and just assumed I would pay.

Make no assumptions. Ever. And always protect yourself. Always.

Acknowledgements

My family is small, but we are a force. I would like to thank my wife, Stacie, my daughters, Emma and Jessica, my mother, Gloria, my brothers, Richard and Randy, and my Uncle Martin for all their support and encouragement.

I also thank Shari Reinhart, who is responsible for this book being written. Shari turned down working with me on the book because she thought I was not serious about writing it—and maybe I wasn't...until she turned me down. She received my finished manuscript five weeks later.

I thank Susan Crossman of Crossman Communications, who edited my manuscript without quitting.

And I send great appreciation to Brian Morris , my lawyer and friend, who has had my back since the first day we met in 2000.

Finally, I give a big nod of thanks to the publishing team at Davis Creative Publishing Partners, who have made this strange process of getting a book published as easy as anyone could have.

About the Author

Michael Yasny has spent more than thirty years working in the alternative financing space during which time he has developed both an extensive knowledge of the many financing options available to business owners and an impressively nuanced understanding around which one to apply when.

Through his company, Money Consultants Ltd., he currently helps business owners obtain the financing they need to grow their business…with just one phone call. Thanks to a vast understanding of—and professional network within—the financing industry he shares his extensive knowledge of all the different financial solutions available to business owners, and then arranges the solution for them efficiently and precisely.

Michael is particularly passionate about helping financially distressed companies pull back from the edge of bankruptcy and navigate their way to the high ground of financial success. And he makes a point of protecting his clients from bullies, whether they be creditors, the tax department, or even their own customers.

Regardless of where a company is on its growth curve, Michael works to provide the financing solution that's right for them now, and which will also serve their growing business needs in future.

On top of running Money Consultants, Michael works as a business consultant and has in recent years helped set up two factoring and purchase ordering financing businesses: one provided financing to the Canadian cannabis industry and the second was a Quebec-based technology company that specialized in shrimp farming in Ecuador.

Michael lives in Toronto, Canada, and you can find out more about the services his company offers by visiting www.moneyconsultants.ca.

.